AAT

Using Accounting Software

Level 2

Foundation Certificate in Accounting

Combined Text and Question Bank

For assessments from September 2019

Third edition 2019

ISBN 9781 5097 8171 3

British Library Cataloguing-in-Publication Data
A catalogue record for this book is available from the
British Library

Published by

BPP Learning Media Ltd
BPP House, Aldine Place
142-144 Uxbridge Road
London W12 8AA

www.bpp.com/learningmedia

Printed in the United Kingdom

Your learning materials, published by BPP Learning
Media Ltd, are printed on paper obtained from
traceable sustainable sources.

We would like to thank Sage for giving us permission
to use screenshots from their software within our
materials.

We are grateful to the AAT for permission to reproduce
the sample assessment(s). The answers to the sample
assessment(s) have been published by the AAT. All
other answers have been prepared by BPP Learning
Media Ltd.

BPP
LEARNING MEDIA

Contents

Introduction to the course

This unit provides students with the knowledge and skills needed to carry out typical bookkeeping transactions and tasks using accounting software. In the modern business environment, processing data and information into accounting software is a necessary task in most finance roles. This unit teaches students the practical steps for processing accounting information electronically and will allow students to reinforce their understanding of the sequence in which bookkeeping tasks are carried out.

On completion of this unit, students will have the practical ability to enter accounting transactions into accounting software and to perform bank reconciliations accurately. Students will be able to enter information into accounting software and understand the main features of accounting software. They will learn how to set up general ledger accounts for new and existing businesses and process the typical bookkeeping entries expected of students at this level, including the processing of sales and purchase documentation, recording bank and cash entries and carrying out bank reconciliations accurately. Students will also learn how to produce reports using the software, and understand the purpose of these reports.

Students must have access to a suitable specialised accounting software package, as part of their study for this unit and for the assessment. Spreadsheet software will not allow full unit content coverage, so cannot be used for study or assessment of this unit.

Test specification for Using Accounting Software unit assessment.

Assessment type	Marking type	Duration of exam
Computer based assessment	Human marked	2 hours

Learning outcomes	Weighting
1. Set up accounting software	25%
2. Process sales and purchases transactions	35%
3. Process bank and cash transactions	20%
4. Perform period end routine tasks	15%
5. Produce reports	5%
Total	**100%**

AAT qualifications

The material in this book may support the following AAT qualifications:

AAT Foundation Certificate in Accounting Level 2, AAT Foundation Certificate in Accounting at SCQF Level 5 and Certificate: Accounting Technician (Level 3 AATSA).

Sage software

Why does this Combined Text and Question Bank refer to Sage 50 and Sage One?

To explain and demonstrate the skills required in this unit, it is necessary to provide practical examples and exercises. This requires the use of computerised accounting software.

Chapters 1 and 2 of this Combined Text and Question Bank have been written using examples taken from **Sage 50**.

Chapters 3 and 4 of this Combined Text and Question Bank follow the same content as Chapters 1 and 2 but have been written using examples taken from **Sage One**.

When working through the chapters, you should only refer to either Chapters 1 and 2, or Chapters 3 and 4.

After the chapters, you should then work through the whole of the remainder of the Combined Text and Question Bank as this can be worked through using either software package.

Do students have to use Sage to complete this unit?

No. Students **do not** have to use Sage in their AAT *Using Accounting Software* assessment.

The AAT recognises that a variety of accounting software packages is available and can be used. The only stipulation the AAT makes is that the package used must be capable of performing the procedures outlined in the learning outcomes and assessment criteria.

Do students need access to Sage software to use this Combined Text and Question Bank?

Students that don't have Sage software may still pick up some useful information from this book, for example the practice assessments.

However, those students with access to Sage will find it easier to work through the practical exercises than users of other accounting software packages.

Refer to the next page for details of how Sage software may be bought, for educational purposes, at very reasonable prices.

What version do I need?

The illustrations in Chapters 1 and 2 of this Combined Text and Question Bank are taken from Sage 50 Accounts Essentials. The illustrations in Chapters 3 and 4 of this Combined Text and Question Bank are taken from Sage One.

Sage One is an online or 'cloud' based program and is quite different to traditional desktop Sage products such as Sage 50 and Sage Instant. If you are using Sage 50 or Sage Instant you should refer to the Sage 50 section of this book.

For Sage 50, many features and functions remain the same from version to version. For this reason, it is expected that this Combined Text and Question Bank will remain valid for a number of future versions of Sage.

For Sage One, updates are more regular and therefore some screens and menus in this book may appear slightly different to the version you are using, but you should be able to work your way through the tasks. A full list of updates to Sage One can be found by visiting the Sage One website:

http://uk.sageone.com

How do I buy Sage software?

Colleges

If this book is used by students in a college environment, the college will need Sage to be available on student computers. This publication is based on both Sage 50 Accounts Essentials, which will be installed from disk, and Sage One, which is available over the internet, and students can use either product to study for this course. If a college is using Sage 50 Accounts Essentials, they may use a different version of Sage or a different Sage product such as Sage Accounts Instant. Sage 50 and Sage Instant packages are very similar in their operation If a college is using Sage One the software is constantly up to date.

Colleges wanting to purchase Sage One should contact sageonepartners@sage.com for other Sage products colleges should contact Sage in the UK. Contact details can be found at www.sage.co.uk.

Individual students

Individual students are able to buy:

Sage One by visiting the following site:

http://info.uk.sageone.com/aat-computerised-accounting

Sage 50 Accounts Essentials from BPP Learning Media. This must be for educational purposes.

Are Sage data files provided with this book?

No. Sage data files aren't provided because the material is written in such a way that they aren't required.

New instances of Sage allow users to access a blank ledger suitable for experimenting. Instructions are provided in this Combined Text and Question Bank that enable a new blank ledger to be created.

Skills bank

What do I need to know to do well in the assessment?

Using Accounting Software is a practical syllabus that is assessed by a single scenario involving accounting transactions in a specific period for a business organisation. The scenario comprises a series of tasks that will be completed using accounting software. Your success will depend on the accuracy of your reports.

The tasks can be summarised as being in three phases:

- Set-up (of accounts and balances)
- Input (of transactions such as invoices and payments)
- Output (of various reports including an Audit Trail)

In order to start, however, there are other practicalities that you will need to know but are not directly assessed within the Learning Outcomes:

- How to launch the software
- How to create a company
- How to correct errors

As a comparison, when you use word processing software you will be presented with a blank screen and before writing your text you would be well advised to plan your layout!

In the *Using Accounting Software* unit the templates are already designed for you within the software package. Therefore your first task is to familiarise yourself with the templates. Then you will know where to enter data.

One more factor that will help you is understanding double entry bookkeeping. While you can operate the software without this knowledge, knowing <u>why</u> you are performing the tasks will help you to master them more efficiently.

Logical approaches to tasks

You will be assessed on:

1   Accuracy of data such as dates, net and VAT amounts
2   Selection of appropriate codes (nominal, bank, customer, supplier)
3   Accurate completion of processes (such as bank reconciliation)
4   Selection of appropriate reports (trial balance, etc)
5   Screenshot evidence of some tasks

Entering data

Accuracy is the key here so it important that any data entered is accurate and complete. It is always worthwhile checking that your data is the same as any data given to you on the assessment as it can be easy to transpose figures, for example entering 213 instead of 123.

Appropriate codes

Understanding double entry principles should help you to select appropriate account codes. Accounting software often contains many account codes so that it is useful to know all the most commonly used codes (sales, purchases, bank, etc). Furthermore, if you know the logic of the coding system (eg, 4 digits, first digit relating to the account category) this will help you to look in the right sequence for the code.

Completing processes

When performing an involved process such as a bank reconciliation, ensure that you know how to check that it is accurate and that it has been completed.

Appropriate reports

Most accounting software contains many pre-designed reports that can be selected. Many can look similar but contain brief or detailed versions of the same type of report.

Ensure that you understand what the task requires, and very importantly, when you preview or print it, look at it to see if you understand it, and if it meets the task needs.

Screenshots

Some tasks require you to take a screenshot of the accounting software at certain points. When pasting into software such as Microsoft Word ensure that it is as you intend and that it is readable.

BPP Learning Media's AAT Materials

Supplements

From time to time we may need to publish supplementary materials to one of our titles. This can be for a variety of reasons. From a small change in the AAT unit guidance to new legislation coming into effect between editions.

You should check our supplements page regularly for anything that may affect your learning materials. All supplements are available free of charge on our supplements page on our website at:

www.bpp.com/learning-media/about/students

Improving material and removing errors

There is a constant need to update and enhance our study materials in line with both regulatory changes and new insights into the assessments.

From our team of authors BPP appoints a subject expert to update and improve these materials for each new edition.

Their updated draft is subsequently technically checked by another author and from time to time non-technically checked by a proof reader.

We are very keen to remove as many numerical errors and narrative typos as we can but given the volume of detailed information being changed in a short space of time we know that a few errors will sometimes get through our net.

We apologise in advance for any inconvenience that an error might cause. We continue to look for new ways to improve these study materials and would welcome your suggestions. If you have any comments about this book, please email nisarahmed@bpp.com or write to Nisar Ahmed, AAT Head of Programme, BPP Learning Media Ltd, BPP House, Aldine Place, London W12 8AA.

Sage 50 – part 1

Chapter coverage

You will be required to prove your competence in the use of computerised accounting software by completing an assessment. Assessments are likely to include a series of exercises, for example, entering customer and supplier details, posting transactions such as journals, invoices and credit notes, and generating and saving reports.

This chapter explains how you might complete the hands-on computerised accounts parts of an assessment. It is by no means a comprehensive guide to computerised accounting.

The illustrations in this chapter and the next chapter are from Sage 50 Accounts Essentials, which is just one of many packages that you might use. We use a Sage package because these are popular among small/medium-sized businesses in the UK; and with colleges, for training purposes.

There are a large number of illustrations in this chapter, so don't be put off if it seems long – it should be relatively quick and easy to work through.

The topics covered in this chapter are:

- Accounting software
- Assessments
- Company data and the general (nominal) ledger
- Customer and supplier data
- Journals
- Entering invoices
- Help!

1 Accounting software

Accounting software ranges from simple 'off the shelf' cash book style software to heavy-duty Enterprise Resource Management systems used in large organisations. Very large organisations often have a system that has been built specifically for them, made up of components from a variety of software suppliers, or written for them on a one-off basis.

Obviously, we cannot even begin to cover the vast range of available software, but we can illustrate the features of a typical package, and the most popular one in the UK among small to medium-sized businesses is Sage.

Sage produces a variety of accounting software and this book deals with Sage 50 Accounts Essentials, from which the illustrations in this chapter are taken. In the remainder of this chapter, we will just use the word 'Sage' to refer to Sage 50 Accounts Essentials.

1.1 Hands-on

The illustrations in Chapters 1 and 2 are taken from Sage. The tasks you are required to carry out are set in the period of January 2016.

Sage upgrades its software regularly. However, many features and functions remain the same from version to version. Some training centres may use different Sage packages or different versions of Sage. The different Sage packages for small and medium-sized businesses are based on common principles and are very similar in their operation when it comes to performing the tasks included in this Text. Some screens and menus may appear slightly different, depending on the age or version of the product you are using, but you should be able to work your way through the tasks.

If possible, we strongly recommend that you sit at a computer equipped with a version of Sage as you read through this chapter. Most of the activities assume that you are doing this and can complete the tasks we describe as you go along.

1.2 Finding your way about: terminology

We'll assume that you know what we mean when we say 'menu' and 'button', but there may be some other terms that you are not sure of, so here is a quick guide. In this chapter, we will use bold text when referring to something that you will see on screen, such as a button or a menu or a label beside or above a box. We also use arrows to indicate a sequence of actions. For example, we might say choose **'Settings > Change Program Date'**. This means click on the **Settings** menu and then click on **Change Program Date**.

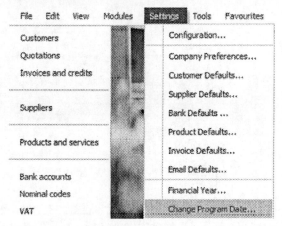

While you can use the buttons on the toolbars as your main starting point, it is useful to familiarise yourself with the Settings and Modules buttons, as the content of these rarely changes, although the layout and position of the buttons can vary between different versions. Here is the main toolbar that you can see at the left of the screen when you open up Sage, with the **Customers** button highlighted.

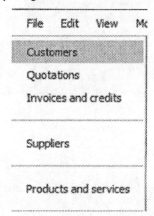

When the **Customers** button is highlighted, the following toolbar appears at the top of the screen.

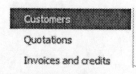

Most of what you do involves you making entries in **fields** – for example the **A/C** field and the **Date** field in the next illustration.

We also refer to 'drop-down lists' which are lists of items to select from within a field. A drop-down list is indicated by a downward arrow button next to the field. The screenshot below shows a drop-down list for the field **Type**, in the account codes area of Sage.

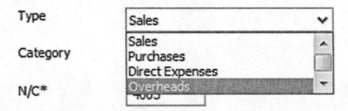

Sometimes you need to select a 'tab' to view the part of the program we refer to. For instance, in this example the **Activity** tab is selected.

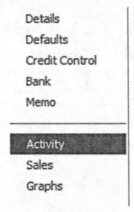

Finally, make sure that you know where the **Tab** key is on your keyboard. It looks similar to this.

Also that you are aware of the function keys (**F1**, **F2** and so on, usually along the top).

Note. On some keyboards the function keys only operate by holding the **Fn** key at the same time. In this Text we refer to actions using the function keys and assume that these will operate directly by pressing them. However if they do not work, you may have to hold the **Fn** key at the same time.

The **Esc** key is also very useful for closing windows quickly.

1.3 Defaults

Computerised packages make extensive use of **'defaults'**, which are the most common entries. When you start entering data you will often find that Sage has done some of the work already, using the default options that would normally be chosen. This saves a great deal of time, but you should always glance at the default entries in case they are not the ones you want. This will become clearer as you start using the package.

1.4 Screenshots

During the assessment, for certain tasks, you will be asked to 'save a screenshot' of a screen to provide evidence that you have completed the task correctly. This means you need to capture and save an image of a particular screen shown on the computer.

To take a screen capture of an entire screen, on your keyboard press **Print Screen** or **PrtScn**. To capture the active window only, press **Alt +Print Screen** or **ALT + PrtScn** (on some keyboards the key may be labelled PrtSc).

The image can then be pasted into a document using an application (using **CTRL + V**) such as **Word** from where the document can be saved as a file (**CTRL + S**).

1.5 Exporting to PDF file

You will also be required to generate various reports from the accounting software. To provide evidence that you have generated the reports, you should export these to PDF (Portable Document Format) files if your accounting software program allows this. If not, you should take screenshots of the full report on screen and paste these to a document. You should save your files to your computer. Reports are covered in Chapter 2.

To export a report to a PDF file, click on the **Export** button at the top of the screen that the report is shown in.

This brings up a box that asks you for the location on the computer where you want to save the PDF file to, and the name of the file. Specify the location and name of the file and click on Save. In the assessment you will be told the location of where to save the file and the type of name to use.

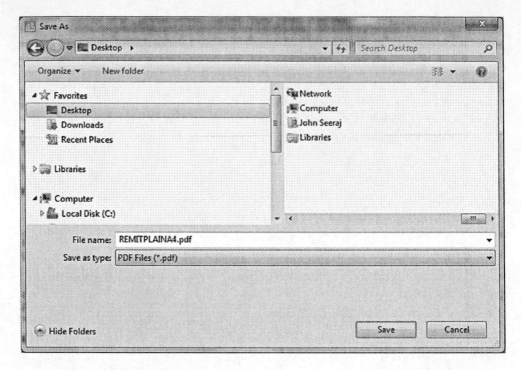

1.6 Uploading files

You will be required to 'upload' the documents or PDF files you have saved. This means that in the assessment, there will be an option on screen to upload files saved in your computer. Selecting this option brings up a box similar to that shown below, which asks you choose the file you wish to upload from your computer.

BPP
LEARNING MEDIA

1.7 Accounting entries

This module assumes you have a basic understanding of double entry accounting, the fundamental principle of which is that **each and every transaction has two effects**.

So for every transaction that a business makes, there must be:

- **Debit entries** in particular ledger accounts
- An equal and opposite value of **credit entries** in other ledger accounts

Ledger accounts are accounts in which each transaction is recorded – there will be a ledger account for different types of transaction such as sales and purchases, and for every type of asset and liability.

The **general ledger** (also referred to as **nominal ledger**) is the accounting record which forms the complete set of ledger accounts for the business.

To know when to use debits and credits, use the following general rules:

- An **increase** in an **expense** (eg a purchase of stationery) or an **increase in an asset** (eg a purchase of computer equipment) is a **debit**.

- An **increase** in **revenue** (eg a sale) or an **increase in a liability** (eg buying goods on credit) is a **credit**.

- A **decrease** in an **asset** (eg making a payment from the bank) is a **credit**.

- A **decrease** in a **liability** (eg paying a creditor) is a **debit**.

In this book, we often refer to 'posting' a transaction. This simply means recording the transaction in the ledger accounts.

2 Assessments

Your AAT assessment will involve a number of practical tasks that test your competence in the assessment criteria.

2.1 Before you start...

Before you start, you should find out from your assessor what the arrangements are for:

- Opening the accounting software and logging in, if necessary
- Changing any overall company details or settings, if required
- Creating new accounts, as necessary
- Posting transactions and completing other assessment tasks
- Exporting and saving your work

Example

The following example is based on a past sample simulation issued by the AAT (simulations were used before assessments).

SITUATION

SFE Merchandising is a new business that has been set up by Charlize Veron, one of Southfield Electrical's former marketing staff. Charlize is an expert on store layout and management of inventories (stocks) and she intends to sell her skills and knowledge, on a consultancy basis, to medium-sized and large retailers to help them to optimise their sales.

Charlize has started her new venture as a sole trader and has taken on some of the risk herself. However, SFE Merchandising is part-financed by Southfield Electrical, and may well be acquired by them if this new venture is a success. Initial enquiries have been so promising that Charlize has already voluntarily registered for VAT and intends to run the standard VAT accounting scheme. (Assume the standard VAT rate is 20%.)

The business commenced trading on 1 January 2016.

Tasks to be completed

It is now 31 January 2016 and you are to complete the tasks in Chapters 1 and 2.

There will be 13 tasks in the real assessment involving setting up data, entering journals, posting sales and purchase transactions, generating reports and so on.

You will be provided with a series of documents such as invoices and cheques. We'll show you how to deal with all of this in the remainder of this Text.

You should now have Sage open on your computer and follow through the activities.

Task 1

Preliminary

This exercise starts with a new installation of Sage or a 'clean' company which contains no transactions.

Your college will tell you how to install Sage afresh or from where to restore the clean company.

If you are studying at home and are installing Sage for the first time on a particular computer, follow the on-screen installation instructions for a standard installation – then **go to the New Set Up instructions below**.

If you are studying at home and **have an existing Sage ledger**, you may **create a new installation and a blank ledger** by following the steps below.

- Click on the **File** button along the top menu and select **Maintenance.**

- Click on the **Rebuild** option and untick all the options on the left hand side. In some cases, you may need to keep the nominal ledger accounts ticked to maintain the **chart of accounts**. This will vary from version to version.

- Once the rebuild is complete, you will be asked to enter the month and year of the company being worked on. This is given in the scenario. If no year is given use the current year.

- Now go to the settings options and overtype the name of the existing company with that of the new company and change the program date if required to do so.

Two important points to note:

- **You will be required to set up a new company in your real assessment. We cover this here to enable us to create the same starting point in Sage for all students.**

- **If installing the program for the first time, you will need to know its Serial Number and Activation Key, often found on the CD or packaging**

New Set Up

The first time you open the package you are presented with a company set-up wizard. A wizard is a type of software assistant that presents a user with a sequence of boxes that guide the user through a series of steps.

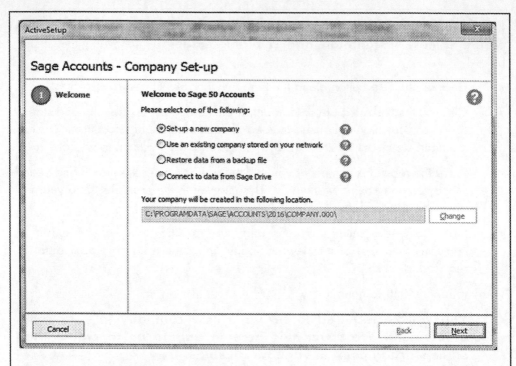

Select **Set-up a new company** and press **Next**.

If your Sage installation does not start at the set-up wizard, you can enter the company information by accessing **Settings > Company Preferences** from the menu at the top of the screen.

Note. Sage generally refers to a business as a 'company' in its menus (eg Company Preferences). However, this is just the terminology used by Sage, and Sage can be used for sole traders and partnerships, as well as limited companies. Where menus and references in this book refer to 'company', take this as meaning 'business' unless otherwise stated. Therefore, such references can encompass sole trader businesses as well as companies.

2.2 Back up and Restore files

It is sensible to create a copy of your work at regular intervals, and at the end of sessions. You will then be able to restore the work later.

Go to **File>Back up** and then choose an easy to find location to store the back up file. The Browse button will help you find a location.

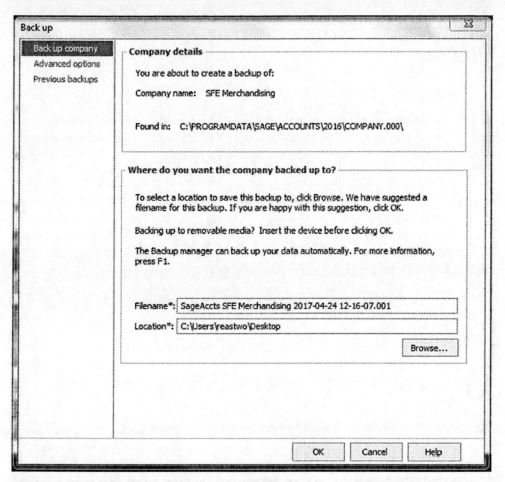

When re-launching Sage software, it will list the last used data files. As below, select SFE Merchandising, being the company you wish to restore.

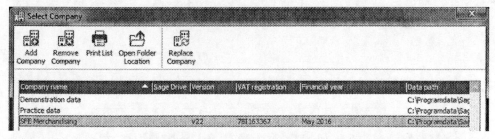

If you are already in Sage and wish to load another back up, go to **File>Restore** and use Browse, or Previous Backups, to find the relevant location and file.

3 Company data and the general (nominal) ledger

3.1 Company data

The name and address of the business should then be entered. This information will appear on any documents you produce with the package, such as reports and invoices, so make sure it is accurate and spelled correctly.

Enter all the information given in the screen below. Use the **Tab** key on your keyboard to move between different lines. Alternatively, click on each line, but this will slow you down, so get into the habit of using the **Tab** key to move from field to field (almost all packages work this way). When you have finished, press **Next** (each time you complete a new screen you will need to press **Next** to continue – you can also use the **Back** button if you need to revisit a screen).

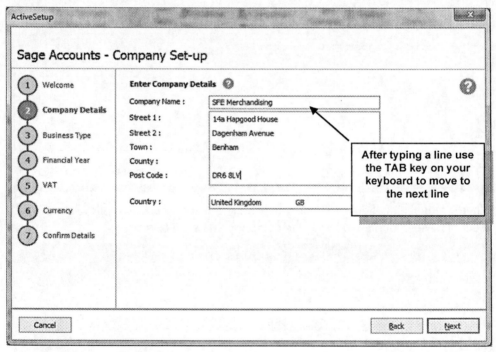

3.2 Accounts in the general (nominal) ledger

As explained earlier, the general ledger is the ledger that contains all the business's ledger accounts. This is also known as the NOMINAL LEDGER and 'nominal ledger' is the term used by Sage.

When a new business is first set up, there is a choice between a number of different 'charts of accounts'. A chart of accounts is a template that sets out the nominal ledger accounts and how they are organised into different categories.

The charts provided are tailored towards the type of business. In Sage 50 Accounts Essentials, you are given a choice between a Sole Trader, Partnership and Limited Company. SFE Merchandising is a sole trader, so you should select this option – **Sole Trader**.

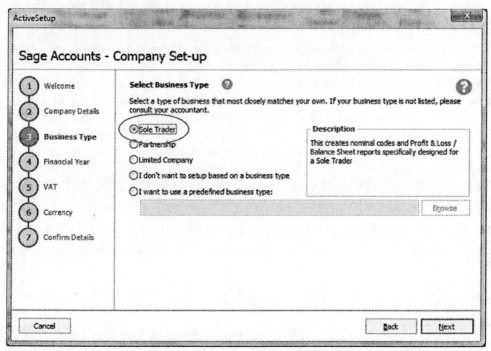

If you are using other versions of Sage, you may be faced with a number of chart of accounts for different types of company, similar to that shown below.

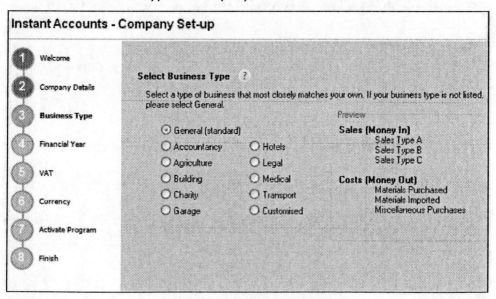

These have accounts tailored for the particular business type.

For example, the 'Hotels, Restaurants and Guest Houses' chart includes sales accounts for 'Restaurant Meals' and 'Alcoholic Beverage Sales'.

Many organisations use the 'General' chart, and modify it to suit their needs. If you are faced with the screen above, choose the **General (Standard)** chart of accounts.

Note that you are not confined to using the accounts that you are given by the program when you first set up the company. Certain accounts must always remain because the program will not be able to operate without them – so you will not be able to delete the main bank account, the receivables (debtors) and payables (creditors) control accounts, VAT accounts, and certain other essential accounts. But you can delete any non-essential accounts (so long as you have not yet posted any transactions to them), and you can rename them and add new accounts as required.

3.3 Financial year

Set the start of the financial year to January 2016. This can be done either by progressing through the wizard or by accessing **Settings > Financial Year** from the menu.

3.4 VAT

The business is **VAT registered** (so select **Yes** in the wizard) and is not registered for cash accounting. Using either the wizard or by choosing **Settings > Company Preferences > VAT** enter 524 3764 51 as the VAT number.

Enter the standard VAT rate % as 20.00.

3.5 Currency

Select **Pound Sterling**, either from the wizard or **Settings > Currency** from the menu.

3.6 Complete set-up

You may get an option to customise the company. Ignore this and click **Close**.

If necessary, activate the program by entering the serial number and activation code supplied with the program or by your college.

The final step is the **Confirm Details** step. Check that the details you have entered are correct and if necessary go back and modify them. Once you are happy the information is correct, click on **Create**.

You are now ready to proceed with entering the company's transactions.

3.7 New accounts and your assessment

You will be presented with a home screen as shown below. There are various options for the purposes of getting started. Ignore these for now. However, if you have the time, there is no harm in looking at these as they contain useful help webinars and demo data.

In your assessment, you may need to add new nominal ledger accounts to complete your tasks. As you work through your assessment, before starting each task, check that the accounts you will need are set up. We recommend you create any new accounts required before starting the task the account is needed in.

If the assessment includes a purchase invoice for stationery, for instance, check that there is already an 'Office stationery' overheads account before you start to post the invoice. The tasks may actually ask you to do this. You can see which chart of accounts has been applied by choosing **Nominal Codes**.

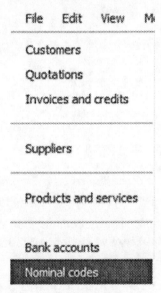

You are then presented with the chart of accounts.

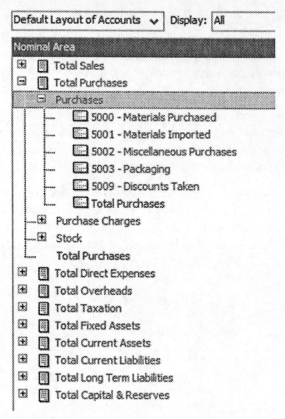

The chart of accounts has been grouped by type of account. These main headings can be expanded by clicking on the '+' sign next to each heading to reveal the accounts contained within the headings. For example '5000 – Materials Purchased' is grouped by 'Purchases', and further grouped by 'Total Purchases'.

If the chart is displayed as a long list of accounts, you can change it to the format shown above by accessing the **Layout** options at the top right of the screen and choosing **Analyser**.

Expand **Total Overheads** and then **Printing and Stationery** and you will see that there is not yet a specific account for 'Publicity material', so we will create one.

Task 2

Create a new account for 'Publicity material'.

Make sure you are in the Nominal Codes function (click on **Nominal Codes** from the left side of the screen). Click on the **Wizard** button

and the program will take you through the Nominal Record Wizard. It is possible to set up new accounts without using the wizard, but we discourage this, because it can very easily lead to problems in the way the program handles your new nominal ledger accounts when it is producing reports and financial statements.

The first step is to decide on the **Name** of your new account (overtype 'New nominal account' with 'Publicity material') and choose what **Type** of account it is.

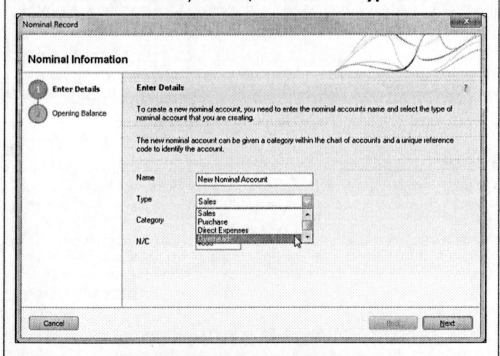

You can further refine the **Category** of account (the options available will depend on the type of account you are setting up – here 'Printing and Stationery') and choose an account code (**N/C**). In fact, the program will suggest a code based on the type and category of account, and we strongly recommend that you accept this.

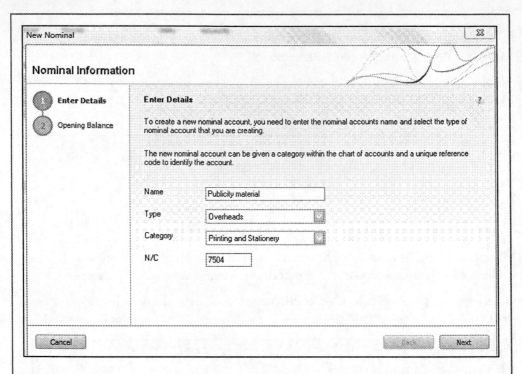

After making your selections and clicking **Next**, you will be asked if you want to **enter an opening balance**. Choose **No** and click **Create**. We cover entering opening balances later in the chapter (directly or via a journal).

Task 3

Vimal was in a hurry to post a transaction. He wasn't sure what nominal account to use, so he created a new account named 'L8R'. Why might this cause problems later on?

It is also possible to change the name of existing nominal accounts. If you are not already in the Nominal Codes module, click on **Nominal Codes**, and then double click on the desired account code. When looking for a particular code, you may find it easier to view the account codes as a list by choosing **List** at the top right of the screen.

The accounts are then presented as a list as shown below.

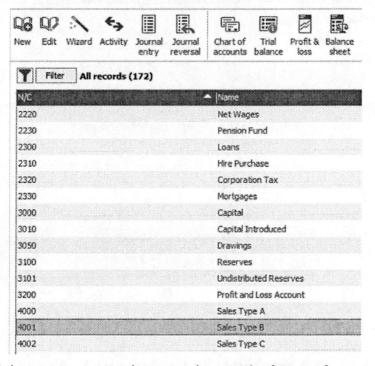

Double clicking on an account brings up the **Nominal Record** screen showing details of the selected account and you can update the name field by typing over the existing name and selecting the **Save** button. (If you cannot see the screen below, make sure the **Details** tab to the left of the screen is selected.) For example, you could change the account '4001 - Sales Type B' to something that is more descriptive of the particular sales to be recorded in that account (eg Overseas Sales).

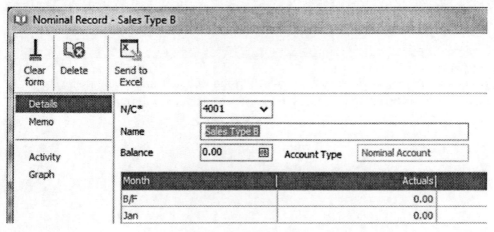

3.8 Entering opening balances in nominal ledger accounts

If you are transferring your business's accounting records from a manual system to a computer system, you will need to post opening balances to your nominal ledger.

Although you can do this using a journal (as we will see later in the chapter), Sage allows you to go directly to the relevant nominal accounts to enter opening balances and makes the accounting entries for you.

To enter opening balances on nominal accounts, find the nominal account you wish to add an opening balance to. For example, you may want to post the opening balance for a property.

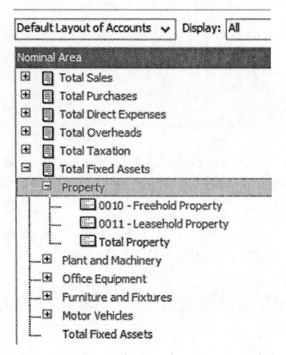

As we saw in the previous section, selecting the account and double clicking on it brings up the **Nominal Record** screen, which includes a 'Balance' field.

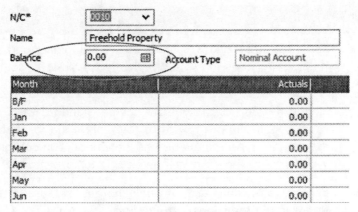

Clicking on the small button to the right of this field marked **'OB'** brings up a screen where you can enter and save an opening balance (although don't save anything now).

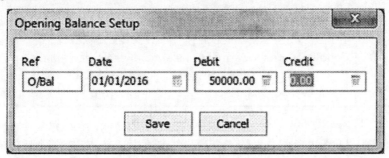

Note that for any entries made using this option, the corresponding entry will be posted to a suspense account. However, since opening balances entered should sum to zero (having the same value of debits and credits), entering all opening balances should result in a zero balance overall on the suspense account.

3.9 Tax codes

3.9.1 Tax codes and VAT rates

When entering transactions, it is important to use the appropriate **tax code** to ensure the VAT is correctly treated. The tax codes in Sage are summarised below. Note that in the assessment, you do not need to know what different rates of VAT are used for. You will be told in the assessment if VAT is applicable, and the rate to use.

Tax code	Used for
T0	Zero-rated transactions, such as books, magazines and train fares. (Think of the code as 'T Zero' – then you will never confuse it with the code for exempt transactions.)
T1	Standard rate, currently 20%. Some standard-rated items that catch people out are taxi fares (but only if the taxi driver is VAT registered), restaurant meals and stationery. You can only reclaim VAT if you have a valid VAT invoice; if not, use code T9.
T2	Exempt transactions such as bank charges and insurance, postage stamps and professional subscriptions.
T5	Lower/Reduced rate, currently 5% for certain things such as domestic electricity, but this does not normally apply to business expenditure.
T9*	Transactions not involving VAT, for example wages, charitable donations and internal transfers between accounts (for instance from the bank to the petty cash account). Also used if the supplier is not VAT registered or if you do not have a valid VAT invoice.

* The code 'T9' would also be used for all transactions if your business was not VAT registered. However, in this case study the business is VAT registered.

As mentioned above, you will **not** be expected to know the VAT rates for different goods and services. However, you may find the following list of current VAT rates helpful in real life:

www.gov.uk/rates-of-vat-on-different-goods-and-services

3.10 Editing VAT codes and rates

Occasionally, an existing VAT rate is changed. This happened when the rate moved from 17.5% to 20% in 2011. This is easy to manage in Sage and only takes a few moments. The process is set out below and is for your general information. If you decide to try this out and change the VAT rate using the following steps, **make sure you change it back to 20% before you continue** through the Text. Alternatively, click on **Cancel** at the end of Step 4 and do not click Save and your changes will not be saved.

Step 1   Click on Settings, and then select **Configuration**

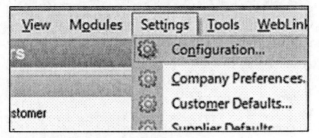

Step 2   Select the **Tax Codes** tab

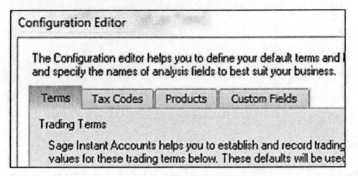

Step 3   In the tax codes tab you will find a list of tax codes. To change an existing code it is best to make the changes on the day it begins to affect your company or the nearest trading day after that, highlight the tax code on the list and then click on **Edit**.

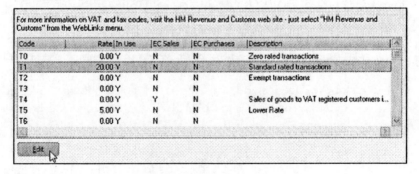

Step 4   The following pop-up screen appears. Simply overtype the existing rate with the new rate (this should be done on the day the rate changes). Once the rate has been updated, clicking OK makes the pop-up screen disappear and the entry will have been amended in the tax code list. Clicking on Save results in the company tax code being updated but you should exit without clicking Save, as we want to keep the VAT rate as 20%.

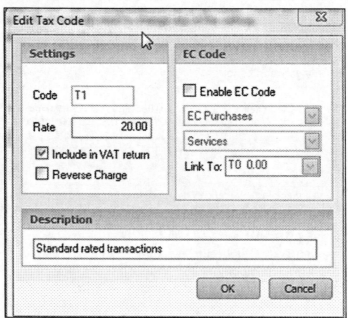

Some companies may prefer to run the older code and newer tax codes concurrently for a short while and in this case, a new code will need to be created. To do this, you would follow the instructions above but instead, at Step 3, a code should be selected that is currently unused (such as T3). The older rate will be entered there, ensuring the **Include in VAT return** box is ticked. Step 4 is unchanged.

If in doubt about which tax code to use when creating new tax codes, check with a manager or your accountant for advice, as all companies are set up differently.

3.11 Trade and non-trade receivables

One thing to note is that the Sage package does not make a distinction between trade and non-trade (or 'other') receivables; anyone to whom you grant credit is simply treated as a customer in Sage. (You can assign different types of customers to different categories and/or to different 'departments', but that is beyond the scope of your present studies.)

Another point to note is that Sage uses old UK GAAP (Generally Accepted Accounting Principles) terminology, rather than IFRS (International Financial Reporting Standards) and new UK GAAP terminology, and therefore uses the term 'debtors' rather than 'receivables'. Therefore, the receivables control account in Sage is named the debtors control account. You will **not** need to post non-trade or 'other' receivables, so you will not need to use Sage's standard 'other debtors' account.

Note. From now on, we will use the same terminology as Sage uses (ie old UK GAAP terminology) for the purposes of navigating through Sage.

4 Customer and supplier data

Before you can post customer and supplier transactions, you will also need to set up accounts in the trade receivables ledger (often referred to as the sales ledger) and the trade payables ledger (often referred to as the purchase ledger).

Note. Customer and supplier accounts are subsidiary accounts of the overall trade debtors ledger account and trade creditors account respectively. Therefore, transactions entered in all customer accounts will be posted to the **one** trade debtors ledger account in the nominal ledger (and the same treatment applies to supplier accounts and the trade creditors ledger).

Once again, we recommend that you set up all the accounts you need before you start posting any transactions.

In an assessment (and in real life) you will find the details you need on the documents you have to hand: the business's own sales invoices and its suppliers' purchase invoices.

4.1 Customer and supplier codes

The first decision you will need to make is what type of codes to use. In Sage, the default behaviour of the program, if you use the wizard to set up the new supplier's record, is to use the first eight characters (excluding spaces and punctuation) of the full name of the customer or supplier, so if you enter 'G.T. Summertown' as the name, the package will suggest that you use the code GTSUMMER.

This is a very clear and easy to use coding system because the code actually contains information about the account to which it refers. If you gave this customer a numeric code such as '1' this might work fine as long as you only had a few customers. However, if you have thousands it is most unlikely that you would know who, say, customer 5682 was, just from the code.

The program will not allow you to set up two customers or two suppliers with the same code, so if you had a customer called 'G.T. Summerfield' as well as one called 'G.T. Summertown' you would get a warning message suggesting that you use the code GTSUMME1. For this reason, many businesses actually introduce numbers into their coding systems. For example, you could use the first five letters

of the name and then the numbers 001, 002 and so on for subsequent customers or suppliers with the same first five letters in their name (GTSUM001, GTSUM002, and so on).

Of course, in your work you would use the coding system prescribed by your organisation. However, in an assessment you will usually be told which code to use. If a task does allow for choice, we recommend an alphanumeric system (a mixture of letters and numbers), as this displays your understanding of the need for understandable but unique codes.

Task 4

Do you think it is possible for a customer and a supplier to have exactly the same code? Explain your answer.

4.2 Entering the account details

We'll now illustrate setting up a supplier account. Please note that the process is identical for customers, apart from the fact that you will be working within the **Customers screens**.

If you click the **Suppliers** button (on the left of screen), this gives you a new set of buttons.

New   Edit   Wizard   Activity   Batch invoice   Batch credit   Supplier payment   Aged balances   Refunds   Write offs & returns

The first way to set up a new account, is to click on **New** and enter as many details as you have available. The details you need will usually be found on the supplier invoice. If the invoice shows an email address, for instance, be sure to type it in, even though you may not have email addresses for other suppliers. Most information is entered in the first three sections listed to the left of the screen **(Details, Defaults** and **Credit Control)**. Take care with typing, as always. When you are happy that everything is correct, click on **Save** and a blank record (like the one that follows) will now appear ready for you to enter the next record. Always remember to click **Save** after entering each supplier and when you are finished click on **Close**.

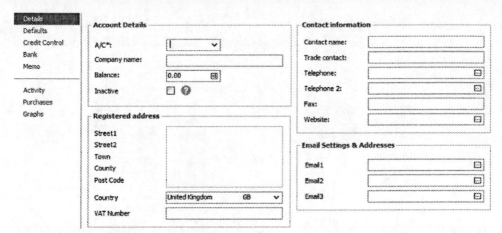

An alternative method for setting up a new account is to click on the **Wizard** button and use the supplier record wizard to enter supplier details. Some people prefer to do this in the first instance, although it can be slower and is not often used in the workplace. Try both methods and decide which is best for you.

Task 5

Set up a supplier account based on the following details taken from the heading of an invoice. Decide on an appropriate coding system yourself.

McAlistair Supplies Ltd
52 Foram Road
Winnesh
DR3 5TP
Tel: 06112 546772 Fax: 06112 546775
Email: sales@mcalisupps.co.uk
VAT No. 692 1473 29

If you use the wizard, don't put anything in for any other data, except for clicking on 'Terms Agreed' in the 'Credit Control' screen.

Remember to **Save** the new account.

You will see that McAlistair Supplies is now listed as a supplier in the main supplier window. Double clicking on **McAlistair Supplies Ltd** from the list will bring up the following screen:

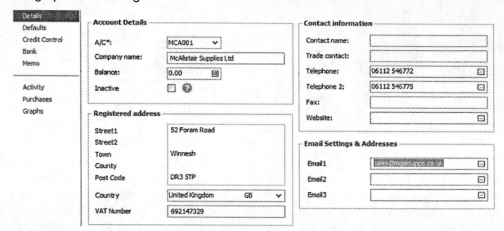

4.3 Entering the opening balance

Earlier in this chapter, we looked at entering an opening balance for a nominal ledger account. The opening balance for the 'Trade creditors' ledger account is made up of the sum of the individual suppliers' opening balances.

You can enter an opening balance for the supplier in this screen by clicking on the **'OB'** icon next to the **Balance** field, once you have set up the supplier. The suppliers you are asked to set up in an assessment task may have opening balances and you can use the screen in the previous section to enter them.

If you see the following message when entering a supplier record:

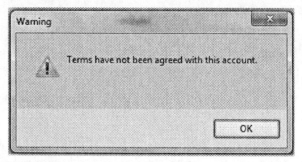

Click on the **Credit Control** section for this record.

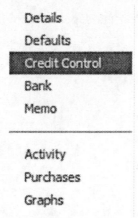

Details

Defaults

Credit Control

Bank

Memo

Activity

Purchases

Graphs

Put a tick in the appropriate checkbox at the foot of the screen, and then save the record. This is simply something Sage requires in order for you to continue entering data for this supplier/customer.

Restrictions

☐ Can charge credit   ☐ Restrict mailing

☑ Terms agreed   ☐ Account On Hold

4.4 Customer and supplier defaults

By default, when you set up a new customer account, customer invoices you enter will be posted by default to the following accounts:

DR   Debtors Control Account (debit gross amount)

CR   Sales Account (credit net amount)

CR   Sales Tax Control Account (credit VAT amount)

For sales, this is probably exactly what you want to happen, unless you are specifically instructed that different types of sales should be posted to different sales accounts in the nominal ledger.

When you set up a new supplier account, the supplier invoices you enter will be posted by default to the following accounts:

DR   Purchase Tax Control Account (debit VAT amount)

DR   Purchases Account (debit net amount)

CR   Creditors Control Account (credit gross amount)

For supplier invoices, however, it would be better to set an appropriate default for the expense for each supplier, depending on the type of purchase. For example, you would want to post a stationery supplier's invoices to the stationery account, but an insurance company's invoices to the insurance account.

To change the defaults, just open the supplier record and click on the **Defaults** section.

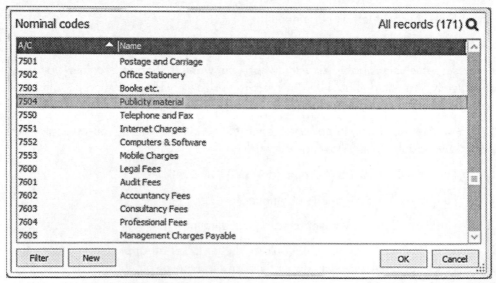

In the box labelled **Default Nominal Code**, you can set the nominal ledger account to which all transactions with this supplier will be posted, unless you specify otherwise when you actually post a transaction. To see a list of all available accounts, click on the arrow 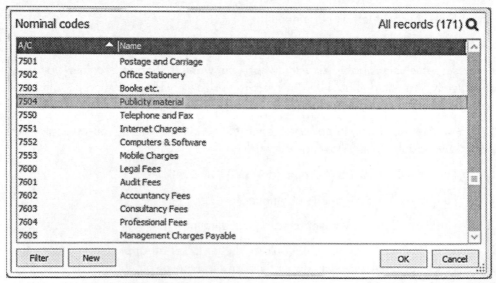 at the right of the box or just press the **F4** key on your keyboard. For example, we may wish to set the default for McAlistair Supplies to 'Publicity Material'.

A/C	Name
7501	Postage and Carriage
7502	Office Stationery
7503	Books etc.
7504	Publicity material
7550	Telephone and Fax
7551	Internet Charges
7552	Computers & Software
7553	Mobile Charges
7600	Legal Fees
7601	Audit Fees
7602	Accountancy Fees
7603	Consultancy Fees
7604	Professional Fees
7605	Management Charges Payable

Nominal codes — All records (171)

Filter | New | OK | Cancel

To do this we would scroll down the list and select the Publicity Material account created earlier (account 7504). If you need a new nominal account to post to, you can set one up from this screen – but we recommend using the Nominal Record wizard, as mentioned earlier.

Payment terms

The default payment terms (ie, how long a supplier gives a customer to pay an invoice) is set to 0 days' credit. If in the assessment you are asked to set up a supplier with payment terms other than 0 days (eg, 30 days), select the **Credit Control** option and enter the number of days in the **Payment Due** field.

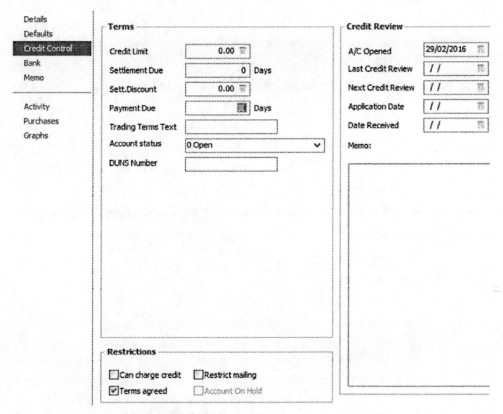

The same process also applies for customers.

Also, a credit limit can also be set for each customer/supplier by entering the amount in the **Credit Limit field**.

Task 6

Open the McAlistair Supplies Ltd suppliers record and set the default nominal code to 7504, Publicity Material.

Remember to **Save** this change.

5 Journals

If you are setting up a new business, the first entries you are likely to make will be done via a journal, to set up any opening balances (although see also the direct method covered earlier in this chapter for entering opening balances).

Journals are also used for non-routine transactions, such as the correction of errors and writing off irrecoverable debts. Error corrections and irrecoverable debts are covered at the end of Chapter 2.

To post a journal in Sage, choose **Nominal Codes > Journal Entry**.

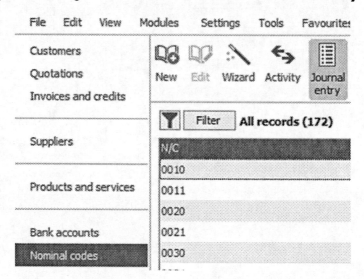

This journal entry screen looks reassuringly similar to a journal slip in a manual system, but all you need to do in a computerised system is to fill in the slip and click on **Save**.

Note. Once saved or 'posted' it is not possible to correct a journal and you will need to input another journal to correct any errors so check carefully before saving.

Let's suppose you want to post the following journal, to set up the opening cash and capital balances.

		£	£
DEBIT	Bank	2,750.00	
DEBIT	Petty Cash	250.00	
CREDIT	Capital		3,000.00

The Nominal Ledger journal input screen is shown below.

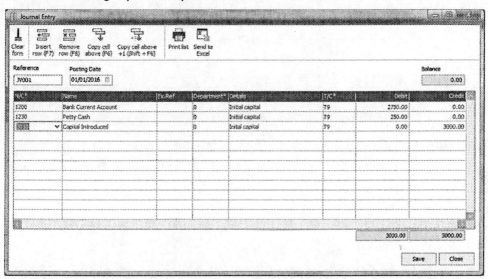

The table below explains what to do as you work through each entry field, in the order in which the Tab key will take you through them.

SCREEN ITEM	HOW IT WORKS
Reference	Type in the journal slip number you are given, if any. Journals should be numbered consecutively, so you may need to check to find out the number of the previous journal. If this is the first ever journal, choose your own coding system and make sure it has room for expansion. For example,'J001' allows for up to 999 journals in total.
Date	By default, this field (box) will show the program date, but you should change it to 01/01/16. Pressing the F4 key, or Clicking the [icon] button will make a little calendar appear.
N/C	Enter the nominal ledger code of the account affected, or press F4 or click the [icon] button to the right of this field to select from a list.

SCREEN ITEM	HOW IT WORKS
Name	This field will be filled in automatically by the program when you select the nominal code.
Ex. Ref	Leave this blank.
Dept	Leave this blank.
Details	Type in the journal narrative. In the second and subsequent lines, you can press the F6 key when you reach this field, and the entry above will be copied without you needing to retype it. This can save lots of time.
T/C	The VAT code, if applicable. For journals, this is likely to be T9 (transaction not involving VAT).
Debit/Credit	Type in the amounts in the correct columns. If it is a round sum, such as £250, there is no need to type in the decimal point and the extra zeros.

It is not possible to post a journal if it does not balance.

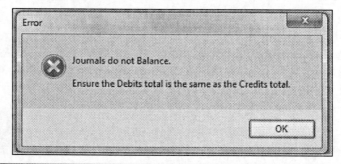

Task 7

Enter the journal shown earlier in this section (DEBIT Bank Current Account 2,750, DEBIT Petty Cash 250, CREDIT Capital Introduced 3,000). Date it 01/01/16 and give a reference of JVI and tax code (T/C) 9. Enter 'Initial capital' in the details field. **Save** then **Close** the journal window.

If you click on Nominal Codes > Balance Sheet > preview > Run

you should see that 3,000 is the total Current Assets and 3,000 is the total Capital & Reserves on the Balance Sheet.

5.1 The importance of dates

By default, Sage sets the date of transactions to the current date according to your computer, but this may not be the date you want to use, especially if you are sitting an assessment.

It is vitally important to enter the correct date when you are using a computerised system, even if you are only doing a practice exercise, because the computer uses the date you enter in a variety of ways – to generate reports such as aged debtors reports, to reconcile VAT, and so on.

If you attempt to enter a date outside the financial year, you will see a warning such as the following.

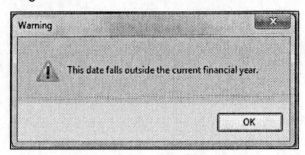

However, if you enter an incorrect date that falls within the financial year, Sage will allow you to do this.

The best way to avoid this kind of error, especially when undertaking an assessment, is to use the facility to set the program date before you enter any transactions. Select the **Settings** menu and then **Change Program Date.**

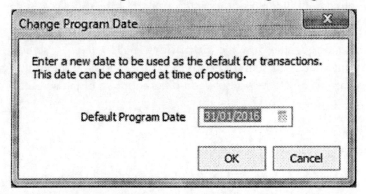

If you are doing an assessment, we recommend that you set the program date to the last day of the month for which you are supposed to be posting transactions. That way, you can never go seriously wrong.

Once you set the program date, Sage will use it as the default date until you change it again or shut down the program. This has no adverse effect on any other programs you may be using and even within Sage, the date will revert to the

computer clock date the next time you use the program. Note that you will need to set the program date again if you shut down and then restart the program.

Furthermore, when viewing reports or lists within Sage, make sure that you have set the date range correctly otherwise they may not show all the transactions you need to see. We will look at generating reports in Chapter 2.

Task 8

Change the program date to 31 January 2016 and check that you have done so correctly by looking at the foot of the Sage screen.

Then close down the program (**File > Exit**).

---

6 Entering invoices

You may be feeling that you have been working hard but have not actually accomplished much yet! This is one of the few off-putting things about accounting software: it can take quite a while to set everything up properly before you can really get started.

If you are feeling frustrated, just remember that you only have to set all these details up once. In future, the fact that all the data is available at the touch of a button will save you a vast amount of time, so it really is worth the initial effort.

6.1 Purchase invoices using the Batch Invoice function

Purchase invoices are created by your suppliers, whereas sales invoices are documents you create yourself. That means that it is usually simpler to enter purchase invoices, so we'll deal with those first.

Having opened Sage, click on the **Suppliers** button (left of screen), select a supplier, and then click on **Batch Invoice** on the Suppliers toolbar. As always, you can use the **Tab** key to move between different parts of the screen.

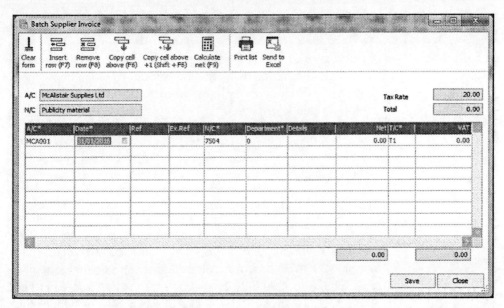

You can enter a number of different invoices from different suppliers on the same screen, and you can also enter each line of an invoice separately, if the invoice is for a variety of items that need to be coded to different nominal accounts.

To repeat the same entry in consecutive lines, just press the **F6** key on your keyboard when you reach the appropriate field.

The following table explains what to do as you tab through each entry field. Pay particular attention to the **Net**, **T/C** and **VAT** fields.

SCREEN ITEM	HOW IT WORKS
A/C column	Select the supplier account from the drop-down list (press the **F4** key to see this, or click on the ⌄ button). The A/C box at the top left of the screen will show the full name of the supplier you select, so you can check to make sure you have the right one.
Date	The program date will be entered by default, but you can change this if you wish. Click on the calendar icon next to this field or press **F4** to see an on-screen calendar.
Ref	Type in the supplier's invoice number.
Ex. Ref	Leave this blank.
N/C	This will show the default code for this supplier (the N/C box at the top left of the screen will show the name of this account). If you need to change it, press **F4** or click the ⌄ button to see a list of nominal ledger accounts.

SCREEN ITEM	HOW IT WORKS
Details	Type in a brief but clear description of the item and be sure that your description will be understood by someone other than you. Usually, you will just need to copy the description on the supplier's invoice.
Net	Enter the net amount of the invoice, excluding VAT. If the invoice has several lines, you can enter each line separately but you should use the same Ref for each line.
	The  button in this field will call up an on-screen calculator.
	Alternatively, type in the gross amount and press the **F9** key on your keyboard and Sage will automatically calculate the net amount. You can also calculate the net amount manually. It is equal to the GROSS AMT ÷ (1 + VAT RATE). For example, £10 gross = 10 ÷ (1.20) = £8.33 net (where the VAT rate = 20%).
T/C	The VAT code, as explained earlier. Type in or select the appropriate code for the item.
VAT	This item will be calculated automatically, depending on the tax code selected. Check that it agrees with the VAT shown on the actual invoice. You can overtype the automatic amount, if necessary.

When you have entered all the invoice details, you post them simply by clicking on **Save**. This will post **all** the required accounting entries to the ledgers.

Task 9

Post an invoice from McAlistair Supplies dated 6 January 2016 for 2,000 sheets of A4 paper (net price: £20.35) and a box of 100 blue promotional biros (gross price: £10.00). Post both items to the Publicity material ledger account. The invoice number is PG45783. **Save** and **Close**.

Write down the total amount of VAT, as calculated by the program.

£	

6.2 Nominal Activity

The first time you do this, you will probably not quite believe that double entry to all the ledgers can be so incredibly easy. To check that a purchase invoice has been posted to the individual accounts, click on **Nominal Codes** and select the appropriate accounts.

Depending on which type of transaction you posted, you should then select either the Debtors Ledger Control Account or the Creditors Ledger Control Account by expanding Total Current Assets or Total Current Liabilities using the '+' signs. Having selected the account you want, you should then double click on it. Remember it may be easier to find the accounts by viewing them as a list by selecting the **List** option.

The screenshot below shows the **Nominal Record** for the Trade Creditors Control account.

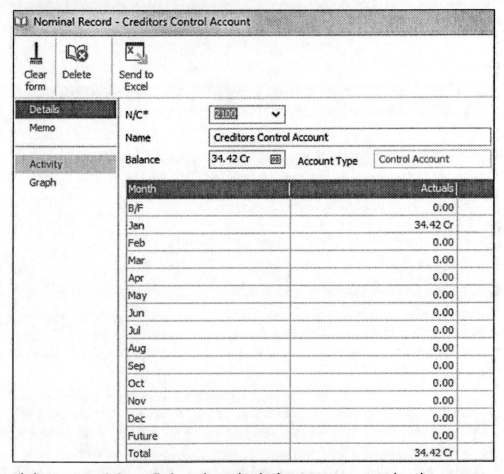

Clicking on **Activity** will show the individual transactions posted to this account, as shown in the screen below.

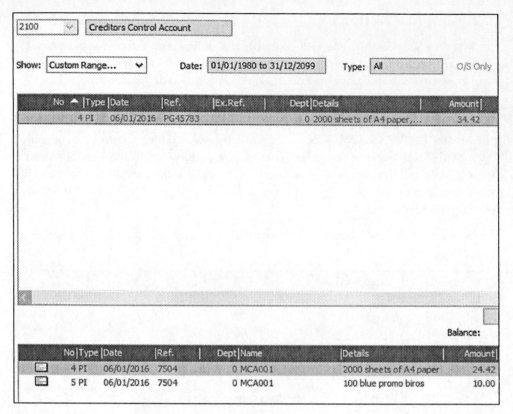

You will see that the transaction has been correctly posted to the Creditors Control Account. But what about the other accounts of the double entry that make up the full transaction? For the invoice from McAlistair Supplies, the double entry should be as follows:

DEBIT Purchase Tax Control Account (debit VAT amount)

DEBIT Expenditure account – Publicity Material (debit net amount)

CREDIT Creditors Control Account (credit gross amount)

You can also check that the transaction has been correctly posted to the Publicity Material account (A/C 7504) and the Purchase Tax Control Account (A/C code 2201) by using the same method as above, ie, checking the **Nominal Record** for these accounts.

Furthermore, to check that the correct amounts have also been posted to the individual supplier account (ie, subsidiary ledger) within the overall Creditors Control Account, select **Suppliers**, then open the record for the relevant supplier and choose the **Activity** section.

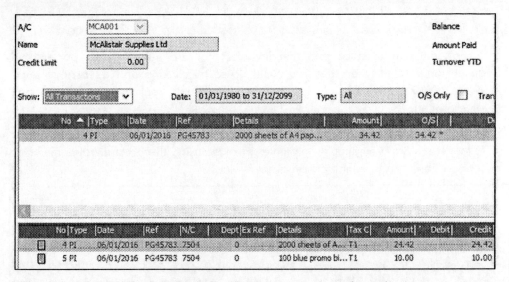

The process for checking individual customer accounts works in the same way.

Finally, if you just want a quick look at the transactions you've posted, click on the **Transactions** from the left side of the screen. This will result in you being shown a list of transactions, numbered in the order in which you posted them. This can be very useful on certain occasions; for instance, if you can't remember the reference number of the last journal you posted, you can quickly check using this screen.

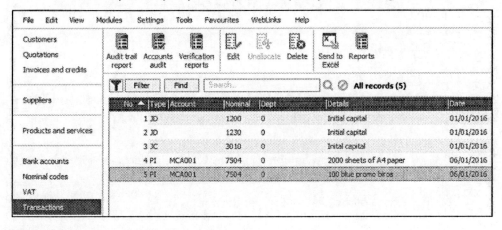

6.3 Sales invoices if no invoice is produced

Some businesses create sales invoices using a different system from their accounts package – for example, using word processing software such as Word. The invoices are then entered into the computerised accounting package.

If that is the case, then sales invoices are entered in exactly the same way as purchase invoices. To do this, click on **Customers** then **Batch Invoice** and enter the invoices in a batch. The batch invoice process works in the same way as for Suppliers described earlier.

BPP
LEARNING MEDIA

6.4 Sales invoices – if the system creates the invoice

In Sage, you can produce printable invoices that are automatically posted by Sage. If you wanted to do this, you could do so by clicking on **Customers** and then the **New** button. The invoice details can then be entered, saved and an invoice printed.

However, in the assessment you will be given a list of invoices or sample invoices to enter. Therefore, you should only enter invoices using the Batch Invoice method described earlier, rather than creating an invoice.

Task 10

(1)   Set up two more **suppliers** with the following details (using the new supplier wizard if you wish).

Widgets Unlimited Ltd
123 High Road
London
W23 2RG
020 8234 2345

Office Products Ltd
321 Low Road
London
E32 2GR
020 8432 5432

(2)   Process the purchase of:

(a)   10 widgets (material purchased) from Widgets Unlimited Ltd for a total net cost of £80. Invoice number WU4474, dated 8 January 2016.

(b)   A computer (office equipment) from Office Products Ltd for a net cost of £800. Invoice OP1231, dated 10 January 2016.

Both purchases attract VAT at the standard rate.

Task 11

(1) Set up a new **customer** with the following details (using the new customer wizard if you wish).

Alexander Ltd
501 Dart Road
Leeds
LS12 6TC
0113 2454 3241
info@alexander.co.uk

30 days' credit (payment due days)
All other fields can be left blank but tick the terms agreed option.

(2) Post the following two invoices (remember, you have to use **Save** to post them) to this customer:

(a) Invoice 001: Product Sale: 10 widgets at a selling price (net) of £20 each. VAT to be charged at standard rate. Date: 15 January 2016.

(b) Invoice 002: Service Sale: Advice on widgets, at a fee of £50 (net). VAT to be charged at standard rate. Date: 25 January 2016.

(3) If you have not already done so, change the names of the nominal ledger accounts as necessary to accommodate the different sales types in (2).

Task 12

As you should know from previous studies, a trial balance is a list of balances of all the ledger accounts. Preview a trial balance at this stage. Select **Nominal Codes > Trial Balance > Preview > Run**, and set month period to '1: January 2016'.

Date: 29/02/2016	SFE Merchandising		Page: 1
Time: 13:04:10	Period Trial Balance		

To Period: Month 1, January 2016

N/C	Name	Debit	Credit
0030	Office Equipment	800.00	
1100	Debtors Control Account	300.00	
1200	Bank Current Account	2,750.00	
1230	Petty Cash	250.00	
2100	Creditors Control Account		1,090.42
2200	Sales Tax Control Account		50.00
2201	Purchase Tax Control Account	181.74	
3010	Capital Introduced		3,000.00
4000	Sales - products		200.00
4001	Sales - services		50.00
5000	Materials Purchased	80.00	
7504	Publicity material	28.68	
	Totals:	4,390.42	4,390.42

6.5 Credit notes

Supplier credit notes are posted in exactly the same way as supplier invoices, except that you begin by clicking on **Supplier** and then the **Batch Credit** button, instead of the Batch Invoice button. The entries you make will appear in red, as a visual reminder that you are creating a credit note.

Customer credit notes can be posted in this way too.

7 Help!

7.1 Help in Sage

If ever you are unsure about how to perform a task in Sage, take a look through the built-in Help feature. Help is accessed by selecting **Help > F1- In Product Help** or just pressing the **F1** key. Then click on **Search** and type in a word or a phrase on the topic you need help with (eg 'Opening balances') and hit the Enter key. This brings up a number of results of help topics containing the phrase 'Opening balances'. The first result should be the most relevant. There is also an **Ask Sage** option in the Help menu. Selecting this takes you to an online version of Sage help if you are connected to internet.

7.2 Help from your manager and others

Whenever you are unsure about what to do, or are faced with an error message you are unsure about, the golden rule is to **ask for help or advice**.

Don't ignore error messages. If possible, have your manager or someone more senior look at the message immediately and advise you on what action to take. If you need to provide details for someone if they can't get to your screen to view it, take a screenshot for them.

Chapter overview

- Accounting software ranges from simple bookkeeping tools to more complex packages. Sage's products are among the most popular packages in the UK.

- Assessments may involve setting up new customer and supplier accounts, posting journals, invoices, payments and receipts, and generating reports or other types of output.

- It is essential to make sure that you are posting transactions to the correct financial year.

- New nominal ledger accounts can be set up using the accounting package's 'wizard'.

- VAT is dealt with by assigning the correct tax code to a transaction.

- New customer and supplier accounts should be given consistent and meaningful codes.

- Using the keyboard shortcuts may help you when you are entering data into Sage. The Tab key, the Esc key and the function keys (eg F4 and F6) can often speed up your work.

- Familiarise yourself with the Help feature; it could come in handy both in your work and in your assessment.

- Never ignore error messages, ask for help or advice from your manager.

Keywords

- **Activity:** the transactions that have occurred on an account

- **Chart of accounts:** a template that sets out the nominal ledger accounts and how they are organised into different categories

- **Customer:** a person or organisation that buys products or services from your organisation

- **Customer record:** the details relating to the customer account, for example name and address, contact details and credit terms

- **Defaults:** the entries that the accounting package expects to normally be made in a particular field

- **Field:** a box on screen in which you enter data or select from a list (similar to a spreadsheet cell)

- **General ledger:** the ledger containing the statement of profit or loss (income statement) and statement of financial position (balance sheet) accounts

- **Ledger accounts:** accounts in which each transaction is recorded

- **Nominal ledger:** the term Sage uses for the ledger containing the income statement (profit and loss) and statement of financial position (balance sheet) accounts

- **Program date:** the date Sage uses as the default for any transactions that are posted (the default may be overwritten)

- **Supplier:** a person or organisation that your organisation buys products or services from

- **Supplier record:** the details relating to the supplier account, for example name and address, contact details and credit terms

- **Trade creditors ledger:** the collection of supplier accounts, also known as the purchase ledger

- **Trade debtors ledger:** the collection of customer accounts, also known as the sales ledger

- **Tax code:** Sage's term for the code to be used to calculate VAT

Test your learning

1 What is a 'field' in an accounting package?

2 What do you understand by the term 'default'?

3 What is a chart of accounts?

4 What must be set up before a supplier credit invoice can be posted?

5 How would a supplier invoice be assigned to the correct nominal ledger expenditure account?

6 If you attempt to post a journal that does not balance, the difference will be posted to the suspense account. True or false? Explain your answer.

7 If a purchase invoice has five separate lines, should these be posted individually or is it sufficient just to post the invoice totals?

Sage 50 – part 2

2

Chapter coverage

The topics covered in this chapter follow on from where you should have reached in Chapter 1.

The subjects covered in this chapter are:

- Payments and receipts
- Bank reconciliations
- Reports and other types of output
- Error correction
- Irrecoverable debts
- Month-end procedures

1 Payments and receipts

Your assessment may include details of payments and receipts to enter into the accounts. These could comprise cash, cheques and payments made or received directly from/to the bank account (eg payments made or received by 'BACS' or 'Faster Payments' services).

You need to be able to distinguish between cheques that you have sent to **SUPPLIERS** and cheques received from **customers**. If it is a cheque that you have paid out to a supplier, you may only be shown the cheque stub (that's all you would have in practice, after all), such as illustrated below.

Date	....
Payee	....
	....
	....
	....
£	....
	000001

If it is a cheque that you have received from a customer, you may be shown the cheque itself.

Lloyds TSB	**30-92-10**
Benham Branch	Date _____
Pay _____	
_____	
_____	
	FOR WHITEHILL SUPERSTORES

You can tell that this is a receipt because the name below the signature (here, Whitehill Superstores) will be the name of one of your customers.

In the assessment, you could also be given details of an electronic payment or receipt, for example, a BACS remittance advice detailing a receipt from a customer.

Alternatively, you may be shown a paying-in slip that may include receipts from several different customers.

Cheques etc.			Brought forward £			£50		
						£20		
						£10		
						£5		
						£2		
						£1		
						50p		
						20p		
						Silver		
			Whitehill Superstores	1468	75	Bronze		
						Total Cash		
						Cardnet	3818	75
			G T Summerfield	2350	00	Cheques etc.		
Carried forward £			Carried forward £	3818	75	Total £	3818	75

| Date | 23/01/2016 | 500001 | FOR SFE MERCHANDISING | 06325143 |

1.1 Supplier payments

When you pay a supplier, it is important to allocate your payment to invoices shown as outstanding in the purchase ledger. Sage makes this very easy.

There are a number of different payment allocations that can occur in both the sales and purchase ledger. Usually, you will pay most invoices in full or take a credit note in full; however, there may be reasons why an invoice may only be partially paid, due to disputes or cash flow problems. These are unsurprisingly known as 'part payments'. Occasionally, you may not be able to allocate a payment or receipt because it is for an invoice not on the system or the amount does not match with your ledger. In these cases, the payment is recorded against the correct account but not to any particular invoice or credit note and these are known as 'payments on account'.

Discounts can be allowed on payments received from customers (or received on payments made to suppliers), and a discount field is available to make a note of these amounts.

Payments allocated to invoices

To post a payment to a supplier, click on **Bank Accounts** on the left side of the screen and then on the **Supplier Payment** button towards the top of the screen (**not** the **Bank Payments** button, which relates to payments not involving suppliers' accounts).

You are presented with a screen that looks a little like a blank cheque with drop-down options which allow you to choose the bank account used for the payment and the supplier who is being paid.

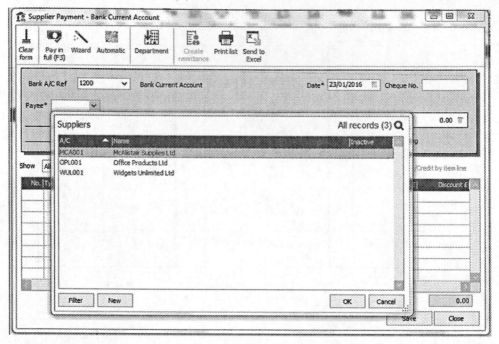

If you choose McAlistair Suppliers Ltd from the drop-down list in the **Payee** field, the next screen completes some of the fields, and the bottom half of the screen shows details of outstanding invoices.

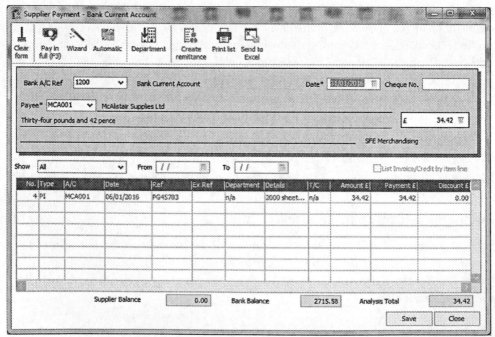

The following table explains the quickest way to post a payment to a supplier. Press **Tab** to move from one field to the next.

SCREEN ITEM	HOW IT WORKS
Payee	Select the code for the supplier you want to pay.
Date	The program date will be entered by default, but you can change this if you wish. Press **F4** to see an on-screen calendar.
Cheque No.	Enter this carefully, as it will help with bank reconciliations. If you are making a payment directly from the bank account such as a BACS payment, you can put the BACS reference in this field.
£ box	Though it might seem odd, leave this at 0.00 when paying an invoice in full, as it will automatically be filled in when we update the Payment £ boxes for the required outstanding invoices to pay.
Payment £	Do not type anything here. Just click on the **Pay in Full** button at the top of the screen. If there are several invoices to pay, ensure you click into the payment field of the required invoice, and click on **Pay in Full**. Using this method, the amount of the payment, shown in the £ box in the top half of the screen, updates each time you click on Pay in Full. The program also writes the amount in words.
Discount	Tab past this if there is no discount. However, if you do need to process a discount, enter the discount amount in the discount field **first,** and Sage will calculate the balance to be paid and enter it automatically into the payment field.
Save	This saves to **all** the ledgers.

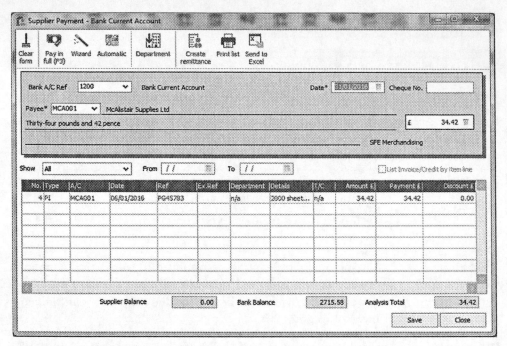

You don't need to pay all the outstanding invoices if you don't want to. You can just click on **Save** when you've paid the ones you want.

This is the quickest way of posting a payment in ordinary circumstances.

Part payments

There may be times when you don't want to pay invoices in full. For instance, you may decide to pay the supplier in the illustration above only £20.00, perhaps because of some problem with the items supplied. In that case, proceed as follows.

SCREEN ITEM	HOW IT WORKS
Payee	As before
Date	As before
Cheque number	As before
£ box	Though it might seem odd, leave this at 0.00
Payment £	Type the amount you want to pay
Discount	Tab past this
Save	This saves to **all** the ledgers

Unallocated payments (payment on account)

There may be times when you need to record a supplier payment but are unable to allocate it to an invoice, either partially or wholly.

For instance, you may decide to pay the supplier in the illustration above only £10.00 but not apply this yet to an invoice(s). In that case, proceed as follows.

SCREEN ITEM	HOW IT WORKS
Payee	As before
Date	As before
Cheque number	As before
£ box	Type the amount you want to pay
Payment £	Leave this at 0.00
Discount	Tab past this
Save	This saves to **all** the ledgers

Click on **Save** and a warning screen comes up asking you to confirm that you want to save the unallocated payment on account. Click **Yes**.

Such payments should be allocated as soon as the relevant information or invoice is available.

Note that VAT is not accounted for on supplier payments. VAT will have already been accounted for when the supplier invoice was posted. Other payments may require VAT to be accounted for when the payment entry is made (see the 'Other payments and receipts' section below).

Applying a credit note to a payment

A further possibility is that there will be a credit note on the account as well as invoices. **Pay in Full** is the answer to this, too. When you reach the credit note line, click on **Pay in Full** and the amount of the cheque will be reduced by the credit amount.

Task 1

Post a payment on 31/01/16 made with cheque 158002 to McAlistair Supplies Ltd for the total of invoice PG45783. Remember to click **'Save'** to effect the posting.

When you make a supplier payment, you also have the option of generating a remittance advice to be sent to the supplier to inform them of the invoices your company is paying. To do this, you use the **Create Remittance** button at the top of the screen, just before you save the payment. You may be asked to generate a remittance during your assessment.

Note. In Sage 50 Accounts Essentials you cannot generate a remittance once you have saved the payment so it must be done just before you click on **Save**. Higher versions of Sage and other programs may allow you to generate remittances retrospectively.

An example is given in the screenshot that follows, where a payment is allocated against an Office Products invoice we created in an earlier task. You can try this for yourself, generating a remittance, but for the purposes of progressing through this Text, you should **not** save the payment.

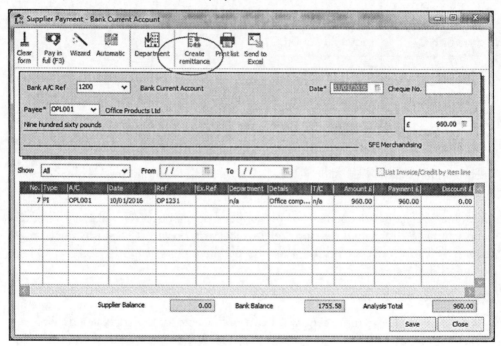

When you click on **Create Remittance,** you will be given a choice of layouts. Selecting the default layout and pressing **Run** should result in a remittance similar to the one shown below.

SFE Merchandising
14a Hapgood House
Dagenham Avenue
Benham
DR6 8LV

Tel :

VAT Reg No. 524376451

	REMITTANCE ADVICE	
Date	31/01/2016
Account Ref	OPL001
Cheque No	

Office Products Ltd
321 Low Road

London
E32 2GR

NOTE: All values are shown in Pound Sterling

Date	Ref	Details	Debit	Credit
10/01/2016	OP1231	Office computer		960.00

This can then be exported to a PDF file and saved to your computer by clicking on the **Export** button at the top of the window in which the report is contained. Please refer to the 'Exporting to PDF file' section in Chapter 1 for details of how to do this.

1.2 Customer receipts

When you receive money from your customers, it is important to allocate the payment to sales invoices shown as outstanding in the subsidiary ledger.

To record a receipt from an account customer, click on **Bank Accounts** and then the **Customer Receipt** button towards the top of the screen (**not** the **Bank Receipts** button). Following that, select the customer you have received money from in the **Account** field.

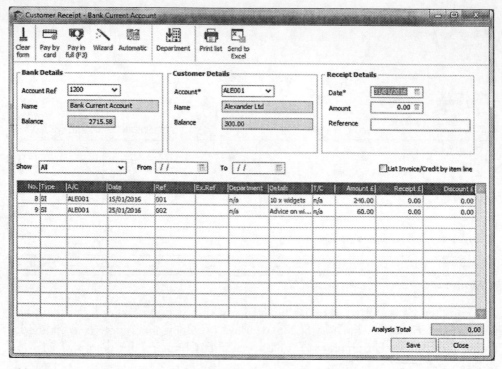

Although this screen looks slightly different from the payment one, it works in exactly the same way, and we recommend that you use it in exactly the same way – in other words, select the **Receipt £** field and click on the **Pay in Full** button, for each invoice you have received payment for. Part payments and unallocated payments (payments on account) are also dealt with in the same way as for suppliers.

One important point to remember when posting receipts is that you should use the paying-in slip number (if you have it) for the **Reference** field. This makes it much easier to complete bank reconciliations, because typically, several cheques will be paid in on a single paying-in slip and the bank statement will only show the total, not the individual amounts.

To recall the details of a payment or receipt that you have already entered, choose **Bank Accounts >** Select the relevant bank account **> Activity**.

Task 2

Post a receipt from Alexander Ltd for £240. This was paid in using paying-in slip 500001 dated 31 January 2016. You should allocate this against Invoice 001.

1.3 Other payments and receipts (non-credit transactions)

Some payments and receipts do not need to be allocated to suppliers or customers. Examples include payments like wages and receipts such as cash sales.

If your assessment includes transactions like this, you should post them by clicking on **Bank Accounts and then Bank Receipts** (for receipts), or **Bank Payments** (for payments).

If you click on **Bank receipts**, you are presented with a screen similar to that shown below.

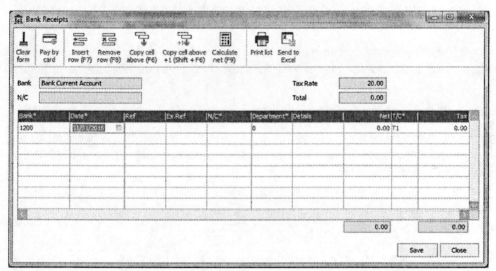

The main differences here to the Customer Receipt screen earlier are that you enter the amount of the receipt directly in the **Net** field; and in the **N/C** field, you select the account where the other side of the double entry for transaction will be posted to. Note that you can split the receipt into different transactions by entering the details in a new line.

VAT on other payments and receipts

Another difference to the customer receipt screen is that you have to specify the VAT treatment of the transaction. VAT is not accounted for on the payment of a sales invoice from a credit customer (a customer receipt) because VAT will already have been accounted for when the sales invoice was posted.

However, for most 'other receipts,' including cash sales', the receipt and related transaction are recorded in this one entry. Therefore you must account for any VAT applicable at this point. Refer to the Tax Codes and VAT rates section in Chapter 1 for the **Tax Code** to use.

In this particular program, if the receipt or payment includes VAT, it is the net amount that should appear in the **Net** field. If you are only given the gross amount

in the Assessment, enter the gross amount in the **Net** field, but press the **F9** Key for the program to calculate the net amount. Alternatively you can calculate the net amount manually by using the formula GROSS AMT /(1+VAT) as covered in Chapter 1.

(1)   The term 'cash sale' actually refers to a sale where the sale and receipt of payment occur at the same time. For example, a supermarket sells goods to customers who pay for them immediately – these are cash sales. The payment does not necessarily have to be in cash. Payment can also be by cheque, credit or debit card. Cash sales differ to 'credit sales' in that credit sales allow the customer to pay for the goods or services at a later date (typically 30 days later). Another example of cash sales is sales made online over the internet.

'Other payments' and 'other receipts' that don't involve sales or purchases (eg, wages, loans etc) do not attract VAT, and the **T/C** code to use in these cases is T9.

Example of a non-credit transaction

Here's an example of how online cash sales might be posted to the accounts using the method described above (don't carry out the transaction). Use the **N/C** drop-down to find which nominal code to use.

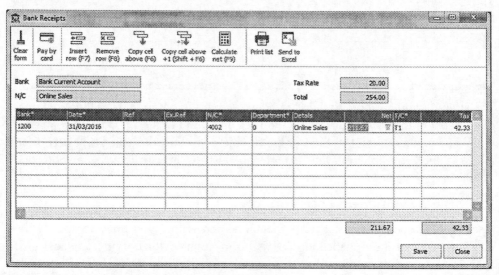

The screen for posting payments such as wages is exactly the same but instead of using the Bank Receipts screen, you access the payments screen through **Bank Payments**.

1.4 Direct debits and standing orders (recurring payments)

Many businesses have regular recurring payments, such as rent and rates, set up by standing order or direct debit. It can be easy to forget to post these – especially as some may be monthly, some quarterly and so on. Sage makes it easy to automate this process. Choosing **Bank accounts > Recurring Items > Add** will produce a screen like the one that follows. It allows you to specify:

- The type of transaction
- Where the debit is to be posted
- Start date
- Frequency
- End date
- Amounts (gross/net/VAT)

Add / Edit Recurring Entry

Recurring Entry From / To

Bank A/C*	1200	Bank Current Account
Nominal Code*	7103	General Rates

Recurring Entry Details

Transaction Type	Bank/Cash/Credit Card Payment
Transaction Ref	DD/STO
Transaction Details	Rates
Department*	0 Default

Posting Frequency

Every*	1 Month(s)	Total Required Postings	12
Start Date*	15/01/2016	Finish Date	15/12/2016
Next Posting Date	15/01/2016	Suspend Posting ?	☐
Last Posted			

Posting Amounts

Net Amount	200.00	Tax Code* T9 0.00	VAT 0.00

OK   Cancel

The screen above shows how the details of a regular monthly payment for rates could be entered. Changing the reference can indicate whether it is a standing order or a direct debit. Note that you may be asked to take a screenshot of the screen above during the assessment as evidence of you setting up a recurring entry.

Task 3

Enter and save the recurring rates payment details shown above.

Although the details for recurring payments are now saved, no transactions have been posted. To make the entries, you have to now choose **Bank Accounts > Recurring Items** to bring up the following screen.

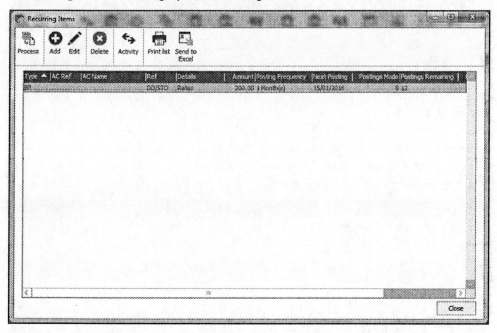

Then you select the relevant series of payments and click on the **Process** button to bring up any recurring payments up to the program date (which was set as 31 January 2016 earlier).

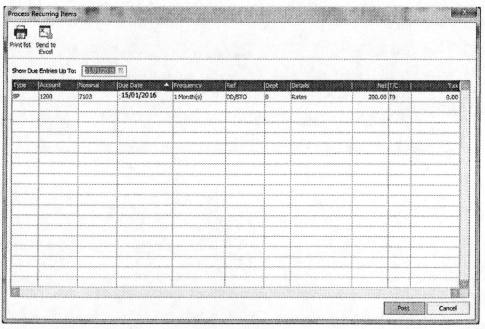

Don't do it now (wait for the next task!), but you can post the payment(s) shown by pressing the **Post** button. You can show all payments due up to a certain date by changing the 'Show Due Entries Up To' date at the top. However, you will only want to post those payments that you expect to go through the bank in the month you are accounting for.

Task 4

Use the recurring payments option to post the rates payment of £200 for **January 2016 only**.

Once you have posted a payment or payments, you should notice that the Recurring Items screen shows a payment or payments have been posted in the 'Postings Made' column.

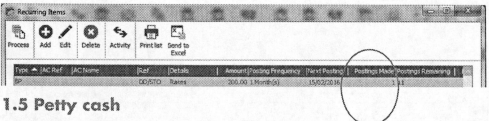

1.5 Petty cash

Petty cash transactions are posted in exactly the same way as non-credit bank payments and receipts (you should refer to the 'Other payments and receipts' section earlier), except that you use the petty cash bank account rather than the bank current account. As with non-credit payments and receipts, VAT is accounted for when entering the transaction for payment or receipt. Therefore take care to use the correct tax code.

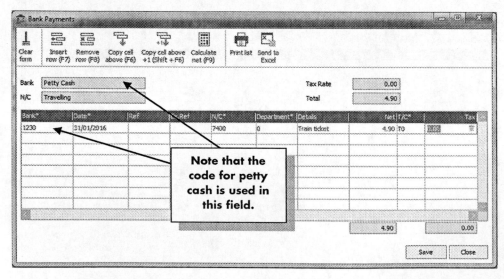

2 Bank reconciliations

As you should know from previous studies a bank reconciliation is a comparison between the bank balance recorded in the accounts and the balance on the bank statement. The differences are called reconciling items and are usually payments and receipts that have not yet cleared the bank account.

To access the bank reconciliation screens, you need to click on **Bank accounts** and then select the account you want to reconcile. In Sage, the default bank current account is account 1200, so you can select this and then click on **Reconcile**. This brings up a statement summary screen.

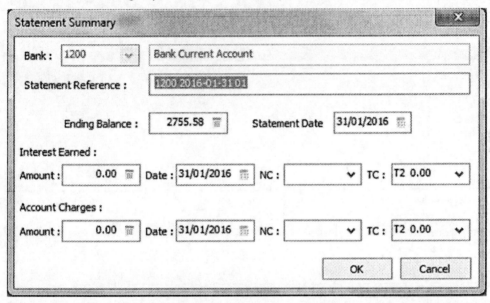

This screen gives you a first opportunity to enter the statement reference, balance and date and to enter any interest or charges appearing on the statement not yet entered in the records. The ending balance that automatically comes up is the balance on the nominal account, so should be updated to the balance shown on the statement.

Say that the closing bank statement balance is £2,790.00. That information would be entered in the **Ending Balance** box of the Statement Summary screen. If the statement is dated 31/01/2016, that can be entered in the **Statement Date** box.

If you forget to update the statement balance or any other details, you can also update them in the next screen (the Bank Reconciliation screen). Adjustments for interest can also be made there.

When you click **OK**, you are taken to the **Bank Reconciliation** screen that follows.

Initially, all cash account amounts are unmatched (you can see the matched balance box at the bottom shows zero) but, by looking at the statement, some will be found to appear there as well. We can match these items. Say that the initial journal of £2,750 into the bank account, the rates payment of £200 and the receipt of £240 from Alexander Ltd are also on the bank statement.

These can be selected and matched by clicking on the transaction and then on **Match >>** (note if you accidentally match the wrong entry, then you can use **<< Unmatch** to go back a step). You can select more than one transaction at a time by holding down the **CTRL** key. The statement screen will then look as follows:

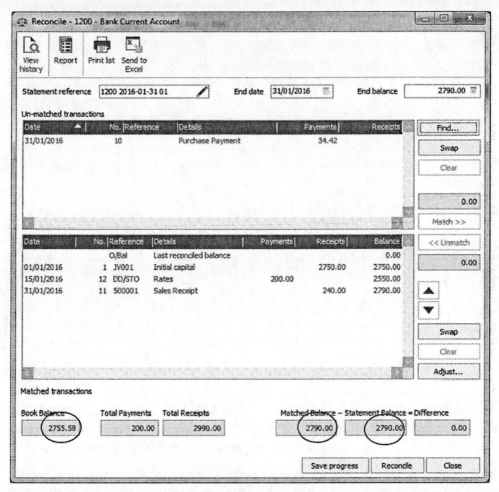

Reconciliation has been achieved! (Matched Balance = Statement Balance) and the unmatched item of £34.42 explains the difference between the statement balance of £2,790.00 and the Sage bank current account balance (Book Balance) of £2,755.58.

(If the book balance does not equal £2,755.58, this might mean that your program date is not set to 31 January 2016. You can check this by selecting **Settings > Change Program Date**)

In order to complete the reconciliation, you must click on the **Reconcile** button; otherwise the reconciliation will not process completely.

The fields you enter in the Bank Reconciliation screen are as follows:

SCREEN ITEM	HOW IT WORKS
End date	Set this to the same date as the date of the statement received from the bank (probably the date of the last transaction shown on the statement).
End balance	Type in the closing balance on the bank statement, using a minus sign if the account is overdrawn.
Difference	This field is updated by the program as you select transactions on screen. The aim is to make this box show 0.00.

Task 5

Carry out the bank reconciliation explained in this section, assuming that the closing bank statement balance is £2,790. Don't forget to click on **Reconcile** when you have reconciled; otherwise the reconciliation will not process completely.

Although we look at reports in detail later in the chapter, at this stage it is worth pointing out that you can generate a bank reconciliation report (a bank reconciliation statement) from the Bank Reconciliation screen (**Bank accounts > Reconcile**). Clicking on **Report** should generate a report like the one shown below.

Date: 29/02/2016		SFE Merchandising				Page: 1
Time: 16:28:15		Bank Reconciliation				

Bank Ref:	1200		Date To:	31/01/2016
Bank Name:	Bank Current Account		Statement Ref:	1200 2016-01-31 02
Currency:	Pound Sterling			

Balance as per cash book at 31/01/2016: 2,755.58

Add: Unpresented Payments

Tran No	Date	Ref	Details	£
10	31/01/2016		Purchase Payment	34.42

34.42

Less: Outstanding Receipts

Tran No	Date	Ref	Details	£

0.00

Reconciled balance : 2,790.00

Balance as per statement : 2,790.00

Difference : 0.00

This can then be exported to a PDF file and saved to your computer by clicking on the **Export** button at the top of the window within which the reconciliation statement is shown. Please refer to the Exporting to PDF file section in Chapter 1 for details of how to do this.

2.1 Adjustments for additional items on bank statement

Even if you have posted all your transactions correctly, there is a good chance that there will be items on the bank statement that you have not included in the accounts. Bank charges and interest are common examples.

For such items, click on the **Adjust** button on the Bank Reconciliation screen, select the type of adjustment to bring up the related adjustment screen (for earlier versions of Sage, you may be taken straight to a general adjustments screen and will not have the option of also posting supplier and customer payments at this stage).

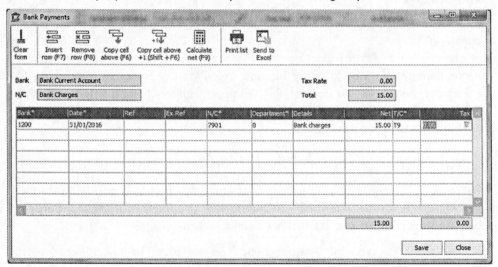

The adjustment screen allows you to enter the amounts and details before saving.

Note. For our purposes, **do not** carry out the following adjustment.

Make sure you use the correct tax code when making adjustments.

Note. On earlier versions of Sage, where you are taken straight to an adjustment screen, you may not be able to use this method to post payments to, or receipts from, credit suppliers or customers because the subsidiary ledgers will not be updated.

2.2 Grouped receipts

As we mentioned earlier, businesses often pay several cheques into the bank on the same paying-in slip and bank statements only show the total of the paying-in slip, not the individual items.

If you use the paying-in slip number as the **Reference** when posting receipts, Sage will allow you to group similar items together when doing a bank reconciliation. This may make it easier to agree them to the bank statement entries.

Within **Bank Defaults** in the **Settings** menu is a tick box called **Group items in Bank Rec**. When this is ticked, consecutive transactions of the same type are combined as one item for display in the Bank Reconciliation screen, if the reference and the date are the same.

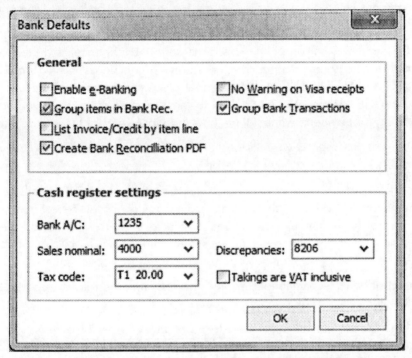

Some versions of Sage have an additional tick box called **Group Bank Transactions**.

If this check box within Bank Defaults is selected, bank transactions (bank payments and bank receipts) with the same reference and transaction date are grouped together within the Bank Activity screen.

To see the individual transactions that make up the grouped transactions, you must use the drill-down facility by clicking on the grouped item.

If you do not want your bank transactions to be grouped together, clear the check boxes related to grouping items. When you clear the check boxes, each bank transaction appears on a separate line of the Bank Activity.

3 Reports and other types of output

3.1 The importance of reports generated by the accounting systems

One of the most important features of an accounting system such as Sage is its ability to provide a range of useful accounting information very quickly. If transactions are entered correctly in the first instance, then accurate summaries or detailed analysis should be available at the click of a button.

To give a simple example of the use of a report by finance staff, the **aged receivables analysis** (or aged debtors analysis) can be generated from Sage (as we will see later) and this will show how old each customer balance is. This will alert staff in charge of credit control to those accounts that are overdue and need chasing for payment, without them having to look back at the invoice dates.

The majority of the reports we will look at are usually produced periodically and used to check on the accuracy of the records.

We look at generating a nominal activity report later, which details all the transactions in a period in each account. A quick review of this report can help to identify errors, for example, transactions posted to the wrong account. The trial balance generated by the accounting system may also highlight errors, for example, if a suspense account has been set up and not yet been cleared.

We looked at bank reconciliations earlier and checking the related report against the bank statements is an important procedure that should be carried out regularly.

The various reports can also be used to gain an overview of different financial areas and as a tool when dealing with customers and suppliers. Areas focused on might include identifying and dealing with overdue customer invoices (aged receivables analysis), seeing which suppliers are due for payment (payables listings) and establishing the cash available to the business to meet its commitments (bank related reports).

3.2 Generating reports

When you have finished entering transactions, the final task in your assessment will be to generate some reports.

Sage offers you a large number of different standard reports. You can also create others of your own if you wish, containing the information you choose. Although the pre-prepared reports that are available in Sage don't all have names that you will immediately recognise from your knowledge of manual accounting systems, rest assured that everything you are likely to be asked to produce in an assessment can easily be found.

One or two reports, such as customer statements, have their own buttons but, in general, to generate a report, you open the part of the program you want a report on and choose the **Reports** button which usually appears on the far right hand side of the menu at the top of the screen:

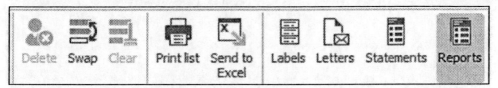

Here's an example of the range of customer reports that you could generate. To get to this screen, click on **Customers,** then **Reports**. By clicking on each folder, you can see the reports available for each category.

Remember Sage uses old UK GAAP terminology.

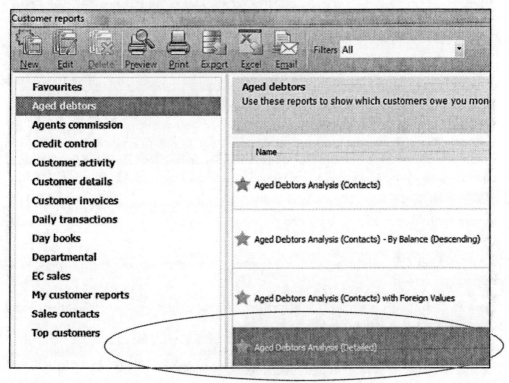

In recent versions of Sage, reports are organised into separate sections by subject, as shown in the illustration. In older versions, this screen is laid out slightly differently, listing reports in folders or individually in alphabetical order. When you have found your report, double click on it or press the **Preview** button.

A screen will appear prompting you to enter the criteria for the report. The screenshot below shows the criteria specification screen that would be displayed if you were producing a supplier activity report (accessed within supplier reports: **Suppliers > Reports > Supplier Activity > Supplier Activity (Detailed)**.

Criteria for Supplier Activity (Detailed)

Criteria Values

Enter the values to use for the criteria in this report

Supplier Ref	Between (inclusive)	MCA001	and	MCA001
Transaction Date	Between (inclusive)	01/01/2016	and	31/01/2016
Transaction No	Between (inclusive)	1	and	99999999
Nominal Code	Between (inclusive)		and	99999999
Inc B/Fwd Tran	☐			
Exc Later Payments	☐			

Preview a sample report for a specified number of records or transactions (0 for all)   0

Help   OK   Cancel

The default settings will produce a report on **all** supplier accounts up until the date specified, unless you have selected a supplier. If you wish, you can specify that you only want a report on a specific account (as in the preceding example), or range of accounts, by making selections in the **Supplier Ref** boxes. You can also restrict your report to cover a specific period by making entries in the **Transaction Date** boxes.

Ensure that the transaction date range you specify covers all the transactions you need to see.

After clicking OK, assuming you selected the **Preview** option, the preview will appear on screen.

Here is the report generated for **supplier** activity based on the information from the screen shown on the previous page.

Date:	29/02/2016				**SFE Merchandising**					Page:	1
Time:	17:12:38				**Supplier Activity (Detailed)**						

Date From:	01/01/2016			Supplier From:	MCA001
Date To:	31/01/2016			Supplier To:	MCA001
Transaction From:	1			N/C From:	
Transaction To:	99,999,999			N/C To:	99999999
Inc b/fwd transaction:	No			Dept From:	0
Exc later payment:	No			Dept To:	999

** NOTE: All report values are shown in Base Currency, unless otherwise indicated **

A/C: MCA001   Name: McAlistair Supplies Ltd   Contact: Tel: 06112 546772

No	Type	Date	Ref	N/C	Details	DeptT/C		Value	O/S	Debit	Credit	V	B
4	PI	06/01/2016	PG45783	7504	2000 sheets of A4 paper	0	T1	24.42	0.00		24.42	N	-
5	PI	06/01/2016	PG45783	7504	100 blue promo biros	0	T1	10.00	0.00		10.00	N	-
10	PP	31/01/2016		1200	Purchase Payment	0	T9	34.42	0.00	34.42		-	N
					Totals:			0.00	0.00	34.42	34.42		

Amount Outstanding	0.00
Amount paid this period	34.42
Credit Limit £	0.00
Turnover YTD	28.68

Here is an example of a **customer** activity report:

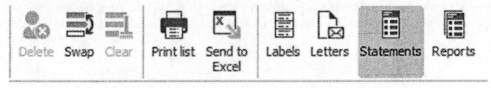

Date: 29/02/201					SFE Merchandising					Page: 1		
Time: 17:14:29					Customer Activity (Detailed)							

Date From:	01/01/2016						Customer From:	ALE001			
Date To:	31/01/2016						Customer To:	ALE001			
Transaction From:	1						N/C From:				
Transaction To:	99,999,999						N/C To:	99999999			
Inc b/fwd transaction:	No						Dept From:	0			
Exc later payment:	No						Dept To:	999			

** NOTE: All report values are shown in Base Currency, unless otherwise indicated **

A/C:	ALE001	Name:	Alexander Ltd		Contact:			Tel:	0113 2354 3241

No	Type	Date	Ref	N/C	Details	Dept	T/C	Value	O/S	Debit	Credit	V	B
8	SI	15/01/2016	001	4000	10 x widgets	0	T1	240.00		240.00		N	-
9	SI	25/01/2016	002	4001	Advice on widgets	0	T1	60.00 *	60.00	60.00		N	-
11	SR	31/01/2016	500001	1200	Sales Receipt	0	T9	240.00			240.00	-	R
						Totals:		60.00	60.00	300.00	240.00		

Amount Outstanding	60.00	
Amount Paid this period	240.00	
Credit Limit £	0.00	
Turnover YTD	250.00	

These can then be exported to a PDF files and saved to your computer by clicking on the **Export** button at the top of the windows in which the reports are contained. Please refer to the 'Exporting to PDF file' section in Chapter 1 for details of how to do this.

3.3 Invoices and statements

Some reports, such as invoices and statements, may be intended to be printed on pre-printed stationery. Remember that when you preview these documents on screen, you will see words and figures on plain paper. This is obvious if you think about it, but we mention it because it surprises some new users.

To produce a customer statement, select **Customers** from the main menu. Then select the required customer and then click on the **Statements** button within Customers.

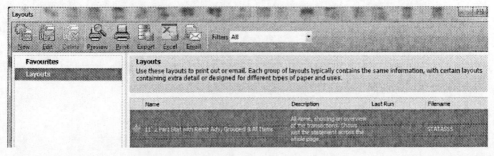

You then click on **Layouts** to bring up a series of different styles of statement.

Using the first (default) option, double clicking on it or clicking on **Preview** will bring up a menu where you can specify transaction dates before pressing **OK** to generate a conventional statement similar to the one shown below.

SFE Merchandising
14a Hapgood House
Dagenham Avenue
Benham
DR6 8LV

ALE001

Alexander Ltd   31/01/2016
501 Dart Road

Leeds
LS12 6TC

All values are shown in Pound Sterling

15/01/2016	001	Goods/Services	£	240.00			£	240.00
25/01/2016	002	Goods/Services	£	60.00			£	300.00
31/01/2016	500001	Payment			£	240.00	£	60.00

This can then be exported to a PDF file and saved to your computer by clicking on the **Export** button at the top of the window in which the report is contained. Please refer to the 'Exporting to PDF file' section in Chapter 1 for details of how to do this.

3.4 Reports in assessments

The following table lists the reports you may be asked for in an assessment, with brief instructions explaining how to obtain them in Sage. Make sure that you select appropriate dates to cover the transactions you have entered. Don't forget to export these reports to PDF files and save them to your computer. Please refer to the 'Exporting to PDF file' section in Chapter 1 for details of how to do this.

REPORT	HOW TO GET IT	WHICH REPORT TO CHOOSE
Audit trail - a list of every transaction entered into Sage including journal entries in order of entry.	Click on **Transactions**, and then the **Audit Trail Report** button.	**Detailed** type of audit trail with **Landscape Output**. Click on **Run**, then you are asked for **Criteria.** Complete these fields, then click OK**,** and you will get a list of **all** transactions in the order in which they were posted
Remittance advice – advice of payment to a supplier showing invoice(s) paid	Please refer to the Supplier Payments section earlier in this chapter for details of how to generate and remittance.	Please see details of this earlier in this chapter
Customer statements – statements of account to credit customers	Click on the **Customers** button and then the **Statement** button.	Click on Layouts and then select '11″ Stat with Tear Off Remit Adv. Grouped & All Items'
Bank reconciliation – a comparison of bank statement balance to bank nominal ledger account balance	Please refer back to the Bank Reconciliations section of this chapter to see how to generate a bank reconciliation statement. Note that the audit trail will show details of bank reconciled items.	Report within the Bank Reconciliation Screen
Sales and Sales Returns Day Books – a list of customer invoices and credit notes	Click on **Customers**, then **Reports** and then click on **Day books**.	Day Books: Customer Invoices (Detailed) Day Books: Customer Credits (Detailed)
Purchases and Purchases Returns Day Books – a list of supplier invoices and credit notes	Click on **Suppliers**, then **Reports** and then click on **Day books**..	Day Books: Supplier Invoices (Detailed) Day Books: Supplier Credits (Detailed)

REPORT	HOW TO GET IT	WHICH REPORT TO CHOOSE
Sales ledger accounts (customer accounts) – a list of all transactions with each customer	Click on **Customers**, then **Reports** and then click on **Customer Activity**.	Customer Activity (Detailed)
All purchase ledger (supplier) accounts (showing all transactions within each account) – a list of all transactions with each supplier	Click on **Suppliers**, then **Reports** and then click on **Supplier Activity**.	Supplier Activity (Detailed)
Aged trade receivables/trade payables reports – a list of balances owed from each customer/to each supplier	Click on **Suppliers** or **Customers** as appropriate, and then select **Aged debtors** or **Aged creditors**.	Choose (and preview) the appropriate aged debtor/creditor reports
Bank payments/ receipts – a list of payments and receipts made from the bank account	Click on **Bank accounts**, then **Reports** and choose bank payments, bank receipts etc.	Bank reports > bank payments (Detailed, Base Currency) Bank reports> bank receipts (Detailed)
Nominal ledger accounts – shows all transactions within each account	Click on **Nominal Codes**, then on **Reports** and then on **Nominal Activity**.	Nominal Activity – * See note below
Trial balance – a list of balances all nominal ledger accounts	Click on **Nominal Codes**, then on **Reports**, and then click on the **Trial Balance** button.	Period Trial Balance

* Note. For Nominal Activity reports, you can set the criteria using the screen that follows to include one account, a range of accounts or all accounts. To include all accounts, just leave the Nominal Code fields blank. To generate a report for one account, just enter/select the same account code in both Nominal Code fields, as shown in the following screen print.

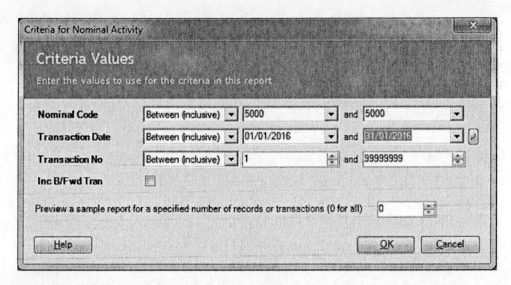

Task 6

Set up another customer as follows:

Springsteen Ltd
223 Home Town
Bradford
BD11 3EE

Process an invoice, Invoice 003, to this customer for £600 (net) for 20 Super-widgets, VAT at standard rate, invoice dated 26 January 2016.

Task 7

You notice that on 15 January, the bank has debited your account £10 for bank charges (no VAT). Enter this transaction to the bank account, debiting the Bank Charges account in the nominal ledger.

On 31 January, the bank credits you with £0.54 interest (no VAT). Rather than net this off against Bank interest charges, you decide to set up a new nominal ledger account: Bank interest received, in the Other sales category, account number 4906. Set up the new account and enter the interest received.

Task 8

Ensure that the program date is set to 31/01/2016. Go to **Customers > Reports > Aged Debtors**.

From the **Aged Debtors** report list, select the Aged Debtors Analysis (Contacts).

Export the report to a specified location on your computer using the default location offered, and a PDF version report will be saved.

Open the PDF version and review your report. It should show all invoices as current.

Transfers

To transfer between bank accounts (including petty cash) choose **Bank accounts > Bank Transfer**. For example, to transfer £100 from the bank current account to the petty cash account, select **Bank** from the menu on the bottom left, then **Bank Transfer** from the task list.

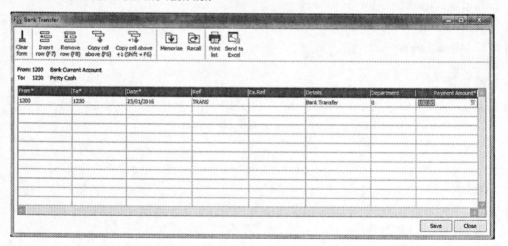

Task 9

On 23 January, you transfer £100 from the bank account into petty cash and immediately spend:

- £20 on train fares (zero rated for VAT)

- £10 (gross amount) on coffee mugs for the office (standard rated). The net cost of the cups should be debited to Sundry Expenses

Enter and post the transactions above. Remember, you can use F6 to repeat entries from the previous line.

Task 10

Extract a trial balance as at 31/01/2016.

If you wish, you can also preview a statement of financial position (balance sheet) and statement of profit or loss (profit and loss account). You will not have to do this in your assessment, but they are easy documents to produce and it seems a pity not to have a look!

Nominal codes > Reports > Balance Sheet for the balance sheet

Nominal codes > Reports > Profit and Loss for the profit and loss account

Your trial balance in Task 10 should look similar to the one that follows:

Date: 01/03/2016 Time: 15:08:19		SFE Merchandising Period Trial Balance		Page: 1
To Period:	Month 1, January 2016			

N/C	Name	Debit	Credit
0030	Office Equipment	800.00	
1100	Debtors Control Account	780.00	
1200	Bank Current Account	2,646.12	
1230	Petty Cash	320.00	
2100	Creditors Control Account		1,056.00
2200	Sales Tax Control Account		170.00
2201	Purchase Tax Control Account	183.41	
3010	Capital Introduced		3,000.00
4000	Sales - products		800.00
4001	Sales - services		50.00
4906	Bank interest received		0.54
5000	Materials Purchased	80.00	
7103	General Rates	200.00	
7400	Travelling	20.00	
7504	Publicity material	28.68	
7901	Bank Charges	10.00	
8250	Sundry Expenses	8.33	
	Totals:	**5,076.54**	**5,076.54**

4 Error correction

If you make an error when you are making your entries, it is relatively easy to correct.

Errors made when setting up customer and supplier accounts can be corrected simply by opening the relevant record and changing the data.

Errors made when typing in the details of a transaction (references, descriptions etc) can be corrected by clicking **Transactions**. A list of all the transactions you have posted so far will appear as follows:

BPP LEARNING MEDIA

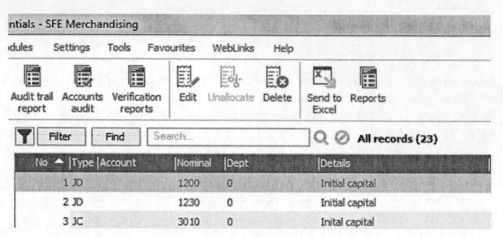

Select the transaction you want to change and click on the **Edit** button at the top of the screen. The following record appears.

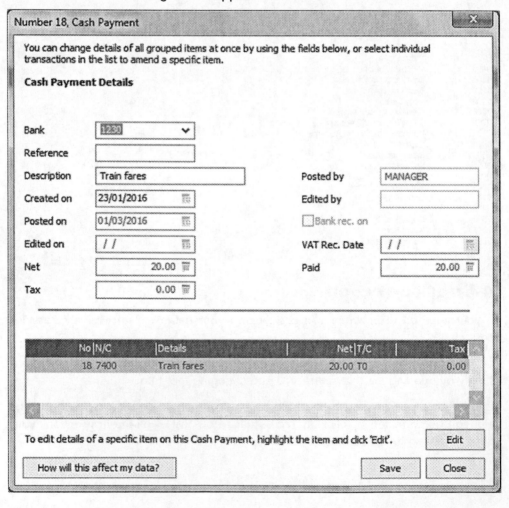

Click on a specific item and click on the **Edit** button (at the bottom of this screen) to change the details as appropriate.

Some corrections that you can make in this way have a bigger effect on the underlying records than others. For example, if you try to change the date or the amounts or account codes for a transaction, the program may let you do so, but to guard against fraud, it will also post a record of what has been changed, and you will be able to see this if you click on **Transactions**: the correction will show up in red.

Some programs do not have the option of correcting transactions by amending the original entry. Therefore, another way is to correct a transaction with another transaction (eg, a credit note, a journal entry), rather than amending the original transaction. In business, this method is also best practice in order to keep a clear audit trail.

Customer invoices

If you have made a mistake on a customer invoice which has been posted, you need to create a credit note, either for the full amount and reissue the invoice, or for the difference. Credit notes are covered in Chapter 1.

Supplier invoices

If a mistake is made by a supplier on an invoice, they will normally send you a credit note, again either for the full amount, with a reissued invoice, or for the difference.

If you have made the mistake yourself, then you need to cancel the invoice, by entering a credit note with the same details. Credit notes are covered in Chapter 1.

Other entries

Other entries should be corrected by journal entry. Students should also be able to post journal entries to correct their own errors that may occur during the assessment. The journal entry is covered in Chapter 1. For a clear audit trail, it is best practice to post a journal entry to reverse the original entry and then post a journal to re-do the transaction correctly.

Task 11

Let's say that the £20 payment entered in petty cash for a train fare should actually have been £15. We could, of course, make adjustments using a journal entry, but here we will use the correction facility.

Click on **Transactions.**

Look down the list of transactions until you find £20 for the train ticket. Double click on that, click Edit, and enter £15 in the net amount. Save the correction.

Now go to **Bank Accounts > Petty Cash** (double click) **> Activity**

You will see that the transaction is now only £15 and the petty cash balance has increased by £5. However, there is a memorandum entry in red stating that £20 has been deleted.

5 Irrecoverable debts

In the assessment you might be required to post a journal to write off an irrecoverable debt.

An irrecoverable debt or 'bad debt' as it is sometimes called, is a balance owing from a customer for invoices that will not be paid, perhaps because the customer has gone bankrupt or due to a dispute. Therefore the original invoice amount(s) needs to be written-off in the accounts.

The journal entry to write off an irrecoverable debt is as follows.

		£	£
DEBIT	Irrecoverable (bad) debts expense	GROSS AMT	
CREDIT	Customer account in trade receivables (debtors) ledger		GROSS AMT

Write off an irrecoverable debt using a credit note

However, in Sage 50 you cannot use the journal function to post this entry, as you cannot post directly to the customer account.

(Remember that each customer account is a subsidiary account of the overall trade receivables ledger account, eg, customer account ALE001 is a subsidiary account of the overall trade receivables account – A/C 1100 – 'Sales Ledger Control Account' in Sage 50),

Instead, you must use the credit note function. This was referred to in Chapter 1. To recap, select the **Batch credit** button in the **Customers module**.

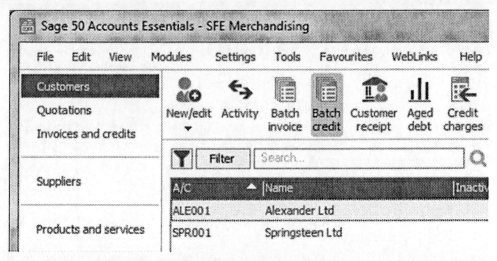

You are presented with the **Batch Customer Credit** screen. The entries you make will be similar to those for entering a sales credit note (ie, selecting **Cr Note** in the **Type** field), but with the following differences.

N/C – select A/C 8100 – 'Bad debt write off'

Net – enter the GROSS amount of the invoice(s) you are writing off

T/C – select T9 as VAT does not apply at this stage.

For example, let's say you received notice that the customer Alexander Ltd has gone bankrupt, and therefore the balance of £60.00 (gross amt) for invoice no. 002 (created in Task 11, Chapter 1) will not be paid. You would enter the following credit note:

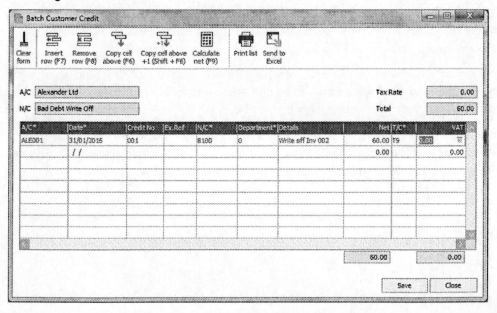

VAT treatment

The VAT treatment above might seem odd at first. You might expect that if you already paid VAT on the original invoice, you can now reclaim the VAT, by entering the net amount, and selecting the tax code as Standard VAT.

However VAT is not reclaimable on all bad debts, as there is a time limit. To comply with current HMRC guidelines, the gross amount is posted to the bad debts account initially, and if VAT is reclaimable, the VAT is separately transferred from the bad debts account to the VAT on purchases account.

6 Month-end procedures

In business there are additional procedures that need to be performed at month-end. The main procedures are:

- Post prepayments
- Post accruals
- Post depreciation
- Close the month to prevent posting of further transactions

You do not have to perform these tasks in the Assessment but it is useful to be aware of these as you will undoubtedly encounter them in the workplace and/or future studies.

6.1 Starting over

All of us can have a bad day sometimes! Occasionally, you may find that you or someone else using the package has made a number of mistakes, perhaps due to a misunderstanding.

If this happens, it may well be better to start again rather than trying to correct all the mistakes, possibly making things worse.

To do so, of course, you need to have made a back-up of the data as it was before all the errors were made. You can then simply restore the correct data and start posting your new entries again.

Back-ups can be made by selecting **File > Back up** and following the on-screen instructions. Restoring data from a back-up can be made by selecting **File > Restore** and following the on-screen instructions.

Chapter overview

- Payments and receipts should be allocated to outstanding invoices, as it is important to know which invoices have been paid.

- Bank reconciliations are very important controls in accounting systems and are easily accomplished in Sage.

- All the reports that you are likely to require are available as pre-prepared reports.

- There are various facilities for error correction, but it is best not to make errors in the first place!

Keywords

- **Bank reconciliation:** a checking process, whereby differences between an organisation's cash book entries, and the bank issued statement are identified. This gives assurance that the cash book is accurate

- **Payment allocations:** matching payments (either received or made) to relevant invoices and credit notes

- **Recurring payments:** payments (or receipts) that are made on a regular, periodic basis. Common examples are standing orders and directy debits

- **Remittance advice:** document that lists all transactions that are being settled by a payment

- **Reports:** form that summarises or analyses data that has been input to a computer system

- **Unallocated payments:** payments or parts of payments that cannot be matched to specific transactions

Test your learning

1   When you receive a payment from an account customer this is posted from the Bank menu using the Bank Receipts button. True or false? Explain your answer.

2   Which report would you run to view the transactions posted to a particular ledger account?

3   Why can you not see supplier accounts on the nominal activity report?

4   Which report would you run to view the invoices and payments posted to a particular supplier account?

5   Transfers between bank accounts should always be processed by using the Journal facility. True or false?

6   Assuming VAT is applicable in both cases; why do you need to account for VAT on the receipt of payment for a cash sale, but not the receipt of payment for a credit sale?

Sage One – part 1

3

Chapter coverage

You will be required to prove your competence in the use of computerised accounting software by completing an assessment. Assessments are likely to include a series of exercises, for example, entering customer and supplier details, posting transactions such as journals, invoices and credit notes, and generating reports.

This chapter explains how you might complete the hands-on computerised accounts parts of an assessment. It is by no means a comprehensive guide to computerised accounting.

The illustrations in this chapter and the next chapter are from Sage One, which is just one of many accounting software programs that you might use. We use a Sage program because these are popular among small/medium-sized businesses in the UK; and with colleges, for training purposes.

There are a large number of illustrations in this chapter, so don't be put off if it seems long – it should be relatively quick and easy to work through.

The topics covered in this chapter are:

- Accounting software
- Assessments
- Business data and the general (nominal) ledger
- Customer and supplier data
- Journals
- Entering invoices
- Help!

1 Accounting software

Accounting software ranges from simple 'off the shelf' analysed cash book style software to heavy-duty Enterprise Resource Management systems used in large organisations. Very large organisations often have a system that has been built specifically for them, made up of components from a variety of software suppliers, or written for them on a one-off basis.

Obviously, we cannot even begin to cover the vast range of available software programs, but we can illustrate the features of a typical program, and a popular one in the UK among small to medium-sized businesses is Sage.

Sage produces a variety of accounting software products and this book deals with Sage One.

1.1 Hands-on

The illustrations in this Text are taken from Sage One Accounting. This is a 'cloud' based program, which is software that is accessed online through a web browser. All data is stored and backed up online.

Sage One is quite different to traditional Sage products such as Sage 50 or Sage Instant. If you are using Sage 50 or Sage Instant, you should refer to the Sage 50 section of this book.

Sage updates its software regularly and therefore some screens and menus in this book may appear slightly different to the version you are using, but you should be able to work your way through the tasks. A full list of updates to Sage One can be found by visiting the Sage One website:

www.uk.sageone.com

If possible, we strongly recommend that you sit at a computer where you can access Sage One as you read through this chapter. Most of the activities assume that you are doing this and can complete the tasks we describe as you go along.

1.2 Finding your way about : terminology

We'll assume that you know what we mean when we say 'screen' and 'button', but there may be some other terms that you are not sure of, so here is a quick guide. In this chapter, we will use bold text when referring to something that you will see on screen, such as a button or a tab.

We also use arrows to indicate a sequence of actions. For example, we might say 'choose **Settings > Financial Year & VAT**'. This means click on the **Settings** tab and then click on the **Financial Year & VAT** button as shown in the screen below.

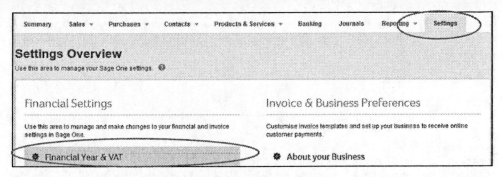

The home screen in Sage is called the **Summary** screen. This can be accessed at any time by clicking on the home 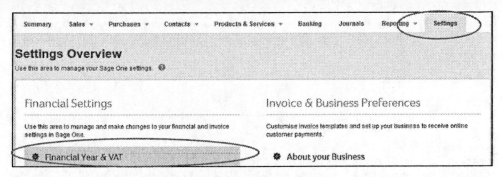 button at the very top of the screen, or on the Summary tab.

The Summary screen is one of a number of menu 'tabs' in Sage. A 'tab' is so called because it looks like a tab in a paper filing system. Each tab represents a particular module in Sage (eg Sales, Purchases etc). Clicking on a tab brings up the main screen for that module, from which other actions are available.

There are also a number of functions available from the drop-down list of each tab, as shown below for the Purchases tab. A drop-down list is a list of items to select from within a tab. In the screenshot below, the drop-down list is indicated by the downward arrow button next to the tab.

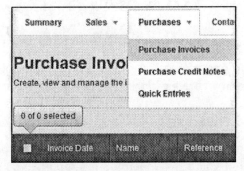

Most of what you do involves making entries or selecting from items in **fields** – for example, the **Ledger Account** field.

Fields can also contain drop-down lists which can be accessed by clicking on the downward arrow button next to the field.

We also refer to 'check-boxes'. These are boxes which when clicked on, show a tick symbol. When we say something like 'tick the check box', this simply means click on the check-box so that a tick appears in the box.

Finally, make sure that you know where the Tab key is on your keyboard (usually above the Caps Lock key). This allows you to move easily between fields and looks something like this.

1.3 Defaults

Computerised software programs make extensive use of **defaults**, which are the most common entries. When you start entering data, you will often find that Sage has done some of the work already, using the default options that would normally be chosen. This saves a great deal of time, but you should always glance at the default entries in case they are not the ones you want. This will become clearer as you start using the program.

1.4 Screenshots

During the assessment, for certain tasks, you will be asked to 'save a screenshot' of a screen to provide evidence that you have completed the task correctly. This means you need to capture and save an image of a particular screen shown on the computer.

To take a screen capture of an entire screen, on your keyboard press **Print Screen** or **PrtScn**. To capture the active window only, press **Alt +Print Screen** or **ALT + PrtScn** (on some keyboards the key may be labelled PrtSc).

The image can then be pasted into a document using an application (using **CTRL + V**) such as **Word** from where the document can be saved as a file (**CTRL + S**).

1.5 Exporting to PDF file

You will also be required to generate various reports from the accounting software. To provide evidence that you have generated the reports, you should export these to PDF (Portable Document Format) files if your accounting software program allows this. If not, you should take screenshots of the full report on screen and paste these to a document. You should save your files to your computer. Reports are covered in Chapter 4.

To export a report to a PDF file, click on the **Export** button shown in the screen of the particular report you have run.

Depending on the type of report, some reports may generate a PDF version on screen directly after clicking on the **Export** button.

However, for most reports, the following screen will appear when clicking on the Export button (eg, for the Nominal Activity report):

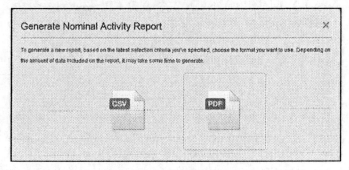

Click on **PDF**; after a short while, the following icon will appear at the top of the screen: .

Click on this icon to reveal a link to the report you have just exported. Click on the link and the report opens in a new window in your internet browser.

Select the save option from your internet browser and this brings up a box (similar to that shown below) that asks you for the location on the computer where you want to save the PDF file to, and the name of the file.

Specify the locaton and name of the file and click on the **Save** button. In the assessment you will be told the location of where to save the file and the type of name to use.

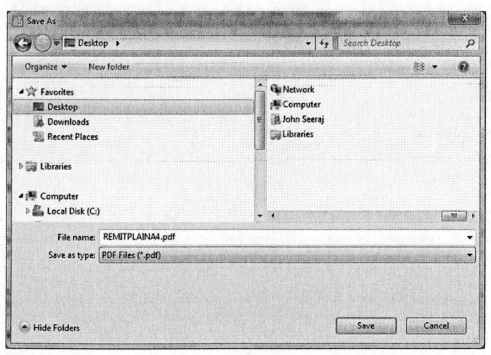

1.6 Uploading files

You will be required to 'upload' the documents or PDF files you have saved. This means that in the assessment, there will be an option on screen to upload files saved in your computer. Selecting this option brings up a box similar to that shown below, which asks you choose the file you wish to upload from your computer.

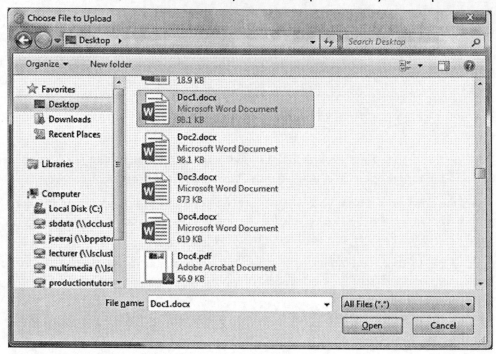

1.7 Accounting entries

This module assumes you have a basic understanding of double entry accounting, the fundamental principle of which is that **each and every transaction has two effects**.

So for every transaction that a business makes, there must be:

• **Debit entries** in particular **ledger accounts**

• An equal and opposite value of **credit entries** in other ledger accounts

Ledger accounts are accounts in which each transaction is recorded – there will be a ledger account for different types of transactions such as sales and purchases, and for every type of asset and liability.

The **general ledger** (also referred to as **nominal ledger**) is the accounting record which forms the complete set of ledger accounts for the business.

To know when to use debits and credits, use the following general rules:

- An **increase** in an **expense** (eg a purchase of stationery) or an **increase in an asset** (eg a purchase of computer equipment) is a **debit**.

- An **increase** in **revenue** (eg a sale) or an **increase in a liability** (eg buying goods on credit) is a **credit**.

- A **decrease** in an **asset** (eg making a payment from the bank) is a **credit**.

- A **decrease** in a **liability** (eg paying a creditor) is a **debit**.

In this book, we often refer to 'posting' a transaction. This simply means recording the transaction in the ledger accounts.

2 Assessments

Your AAT assessment will involve a number of practical tasks that test your competence in the assessment criteria.

2.1 Before you start ...

Before you start, you should find out from your assessor what the arrangements are for:

- Opening the accounting software and signing in, if necessary
- Changing any overall business details or settings, if required
- Creating new accounts, as necessary
- Posting transactions and completing other assessment tasks
- Saving and exporting your work

Example

The following example is based on a past sample simulation issued by the AAT (simulations were used before assessments).

Situation

SFE Merchandising is a new business that has been set up by Charlize Veron, one of Southfield Electrical's former marketing staff. Charlize is an expert on store layout and management of inventories (stocks) and she intends to sell her skills and knowledge, on a consultancy basis, to medium-sized and large retailers to help them to optimise their sales.

Charlize has started her new venture as a sole trader and has taken on some of the risk herself. However, SFE Merchandising is part-financed by Southfield Electrical, and may well be acquired by them if this new venture is a success. Initial enquiries have been so promising that Charlize has already voluntarily registered for VAT and intends to run the standard VAT accounting scheme. (Assume the standard VAT rate is 20%.)

The business commenced trading on 1 January 2016.

Tasks to be completed

It is now 31 January 2016 and you are to complete the tasks in Chapters 3 and 4.

There will be 13 tasks in the real assessment involving setting up data, entering journals, posting sales and purchase transactions, generating reports and so on.

You will be provided with a series of documents such as invoices and cheques. We'll show you how to deal with all of this in the remainder of this Text.

You should now have Sage One open on your computer and follow through the activities.

Task 1

Signing-in

It is assumed at this point that you have already signed up to the Sage One service. (You can sign up either through your college, or if you are an individual student, by visiting http://info.uk.sageone.com/aat-computerised-accounting)

Sign in to Sage One by visiting the following web address:

https://app.sageone.com/login

or through your learning provider's direct login mechanism.

Enter the email address that you used to sign up to Sage One, your password, and click on the **Sign in** button.

This exercise starts with a new instance of Sage One or a 'clean' business which contains no transactions. At this point, your college should be able to tell you how to start Sage One afresh with a clean business.

If you are studying at home and are using Sage for the first time, you will be presented with a 'business set-up wizard' and will need to enter certain details; go straight to the 'New Set-Up' section below to do this. Otherwise, you will be presented with the **Summary** screen, as shown in the 'Start' section below.

Resetting Data

If you are studying at home and are already using Sage One with existing data, you may start afresh by resetting the data by clicking on the Settings ⚙ button. Then select Service **Settings > Manage Your Data >** Tick the **'I understand'** box to confirm acceptance of resetting your data > Enter the email address you used to sign up **> Reset data**.

Important points to note:

• **You will be required to set up a new business in your real assessment. We cover this here to enable us to create the same starting point in Sage for all students.**

• **Make sure you don't confuse this Settings button with the Settings tab; which is frequently referred to in these chapters.**

New Set-Up

The first time you sign in to Sage One you are presented with a business set-up wizard. A wizard is a type of software assistant that presents a user with a sequence of boxes that guide the user through a series of steps.

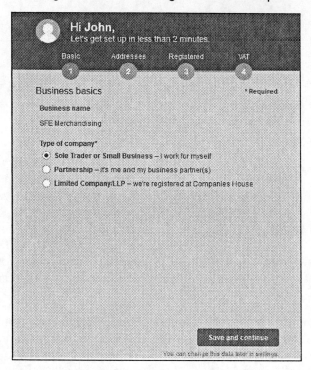

In this series of steps, you should specify/enter the following details, and click on **Save and continue** for each step:

Type of business:	Sole Trader or Small Business
Business Trading Address:	14b Hapgood House,
	Dagenham Avenue,
	Benham
	DR6 8LV
	United Kingdom
VAT Tax Scheme:	Standard
VAT Number:	524 3764 5 1

Start

At this point it is assumed that you have entered the details required when you first signed up to Sage, and have reset any existing data.

You are presented with the following Summary screen, which is essentially the home screen for this program. This screen can be accessed at any time by clicking on the Summary tab, or on the home 🏠 button at the top of the screen. To sign out of the program, click on the sign out 🔓 button, also at the top of the screen.

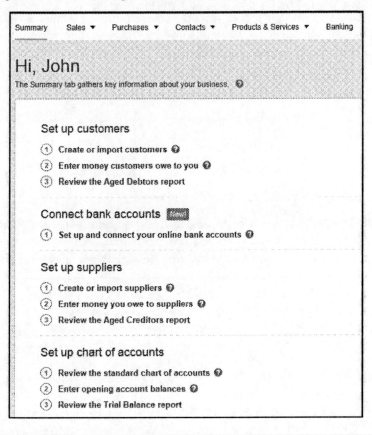

Important note: Sage generally refers to a 'business' in its functions. Such references can encompass sole trader businesses as well as companies.

3 Business data and the general (nominal) ledger

3.1 Business data

If for any reason, you did not enter your full business details using the Business setup wizard described in Task 1, you can do this now by selecting **Settings > About your Business**.

In the **About your business** screen, the **Business name** defaults to the name you registered with Sage One.

At the time of print, this can only be changed by contacting Sage who will do it for you. If this function is still not available when you read this book, it is fine to leave

the name as it is, as this will not affect your ability to work through the chapters. Otherwise you can change it to the name below.

The address of the business should also be entered. This information will appear on any documents you produce with the software, such as reports and invoices, so make sure it is accurate and spelled correctly.

Enter or select the following information if you did not already do so when you first signed up to Sage:

Business name: SFE Merchandising

Address: 14b Hapgood House, Dagenham Avenue,

                      Benham, DR6 8LV, United Kingdom

Type of business: Sole trader or Small Business

Use the **Tab** key on your keyboard to move between different lines. Alternatively, click on each line, but this will slow you down, so get into the habit of using the **Tab** key to move from field to field. When you have finished, click on **Save**.

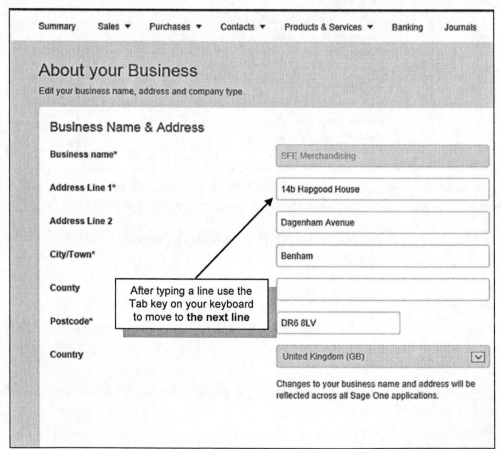

3.2 Financial year & VAT

The Financial Settings screen allows you to enter the financial year and VAT settings. This can be found by clicking on the **Settings** tab and selecting **Financial Year & VAT**.

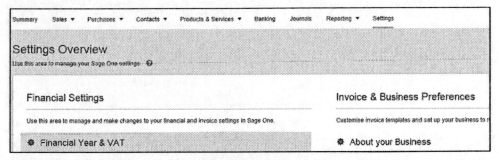

This brings up the **Financial Settings** screen, as shown below. Set the **Year End Date** to 31/12/2016 and the **Accounts Start Date** to 01/01/2016 as shown below. Ignore Year End Lockdown. This function prevents transactions being entered before a specific date.

Financial Settings
Record your financial details such as your VAT scheme details, financial year end and

Year End Date	31/12/2016
Year End Lockdown	
Accounts Start Date	01/01/2016

Our example business is **VAT registered** and is registered for the **Standard** VAT Scheme. If you have not already specified the VAT Scheme and VAT number when you first signed up to Sage, select 'Standard' from the drop-down list in the **VAT Scheme** field, and enter 524 3764 51 as the VAT number, as shown below. Submission Frequency is not relevant for this module; however, you can enter quarterly, as this is a common frequency for most businesses.

counting transactions. ?	
VAT Scheme	Standard
Submission Frequency	Quarterly
VAT Number	GB 524376451

Once you have completed this screen, click on **Save**. You are now ready to proceed with entering the business's transactions.

3.3 New accounts and your assessment

In your assessment, you may need to add new nominal ledger accounts to complete your tasks, or you may not. As you work through your assessment, before starting each task, check that the accounts you will need are set up. We recommend you create any new accounts required before starting the task the account is needed in.

If the assessment includes a purchase invoice for stationery, for instance, check that there is already an 'Office stationery' account (in the Overheads category) before you start to post the invoice. The tasks may actually ask you to do this.

To access the **Chart of Accounts** (a list of nominal ledger accounts) screen, click the **Settings** tab. This brings up the **Settings Overview** screen (as shown in the 'Financial year and VAT' section above). Then click on the **Chart of Accounts** button.

You are presented with the default chart of accounts for this program, as shown in the screen below. The list of accounts can be shown in order of the **Nominal Code** heading as show below, but can be ordered by any of the headings in the list by clicking on a particular heading.

The nominal ledger accounts are categorised by account type (eg Fixed Assets, Current Assets). This is shown in the **Category** heading in the screen below. The categories of account types are grouped by asset, liability, income, expenditure or capital account. This is shown in in the **Category Group** heading in the screen below.

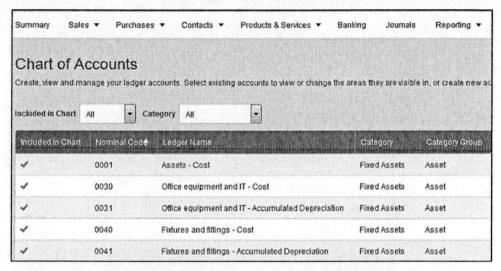

You can search for a specific ledger account in the search box by entering the first few digits of the nominal code or first few letters of the ledger name.

For example, if you enter 'Sales Type A' in the search box, the list shows this account only, as shown below.

If you search for an account for 'Publicity material', you will see that it is not there, so we will create one.

Task 2

Create a new account for 'Publicity material'.

In the **Chart of Accounts** screen, click on the **New Ledger Account** button:

New Ledger Account

In the **New Ledger Account** box that follows, enter 'Publicity material' in both the **Ledger Name** and **Display Name** fields.

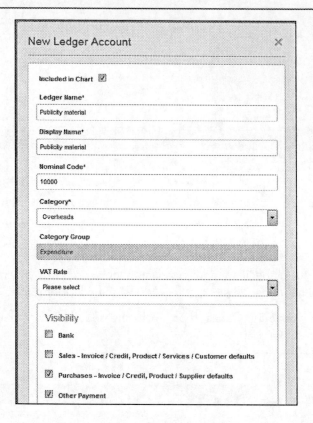

New Ledger Account ×

Included in Chart ☑

Ledger Name*

Publicity material

Display Name*

Publicity material

Nominal Code*

10000

Category*

Overheads

Category Group

Expenditure

VAT Rate

Please select

Visibility

☐ Bank

☐ Sales – Invoice / Credit, Product / Services / Customer defaults

☑ Purchases – Invoice / Credit, Product / Supplier defaults

☑ Other Payment

You can choose a **Nominal Cod**e (account code). It is best practice to group certain types of nominal codes in a particular range within the chart of accounts.

For example, in this program, the nominal codes 4000 to 4999 are available for income accounts. However, when you create a new nominal code, the program will suggest a default code outside these ranges; from 10000 onwards.

You can overwrite this with a code of your choice but, for the purposes of getting through these tasks, we recommend you accept the code given. You don't need to worry about the grouping of nominal codes for this module, but it is important to be aware that in real life, charts of accounts will usually follow a logical structure to facilitate easier reporting and production of accounts. (This is why income accounts are in the range 4000 to 4999 in this program).

You can further refine the **Category** of account (The options available will depend on the type of account you are setting up.)Publicity material is part of overheads, so choose 'Overheads'.

The **Category group** field automatically populates based on the category you have chosen. In this case it is 'Expenditure'.

Ignore the **VAT Rate** for now. In this Text, we will not set a default VAT rate for a ledger account. We will instead select the VAT rate at the time of entering a transaction, since this is required for the assessment. Furthermore, different types of goods or services may have different VAT rates.

The **Visibility** check boxes are automatically populated based on the selections you have made above and you do not need to change anything here at this point. However, if you find that an account is not available to select from in a particular function, this could mean that it is not visible within that function. To make it visible, you should edit the ledger account (described in the section under Task 3 below) and make sure the relevant function is ticked in the **Visibility** section.

After making your selections, click on **Save**. You will now see the account in the **Chart of Accounts** screen (**Settings > Chart of Accounts**).

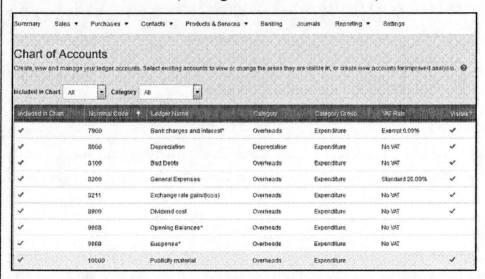

We cover entering opening balances later in the chapter. The options for entering opening balances are also covered in Sage Help. The help page is online and can be accessed by clicking the help button ⊙ at the top of the screen. You can search for a particular topic in the search box, or there are a number of help categories and topics to select from.

Task 3

Vimal was in a hurry to post a transaction and wasn't sure what nominal account to use, so he created a new account named 'L8R'. Why might this cause problems later on?

It is also possible to change the name of existing nominal accounts. To do this, you need to select the account you want to change from the **Chart of Accounts** screen. This brings up the **Edit Ledger Account** screen showing details of the selected account. In this screen, you can update the name fields. For example, you could change 'Sales Type A' to something that is more descriptive of the particular sales to be recorded in that account, eg 'Overseas Sales', although don't save anything now.

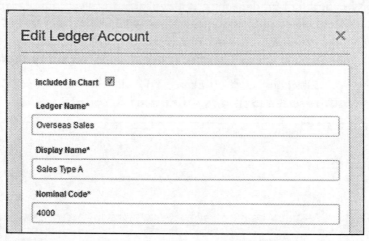

3.4 Entering opening balances in nominal ledger accounts

If you are transferring your business's accounting records from a manual system to a computer system, you will need to post opening balances to your nominal ledger.

Sage One allows you to go directly to the relevant nominal ledger accounts to enter opening balances, and makes the accounting entries for you when you save these. This can be a useful method to use the assessment.

To access the **Nominal Opening Balances** screen, choose **Settings > Nominal Opening Balances**. For example, you may want to post the opening balance for the 'Fixtures and Fittings – Cost' account.

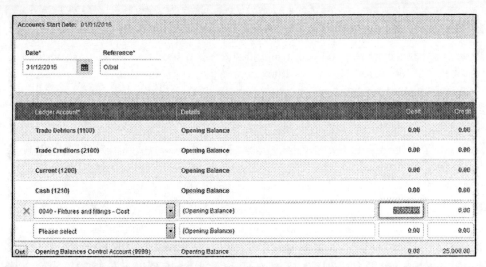

You can enter the opening balance by selecting the Fixtures and Fittings - Cost account from the ledger account field drop-down list and entering the opening balance figure in the appropriate debit or credit field, as shown. This can be posted by clicking on Save (although don't save anything now).

Note. This program requires the opening balances to be created on the date before the accounts start date (see the 'Financial Year & VAT' section to set the accounts start date). This is in order to separate the opening balance from any transactions that occur on the first day of the accounting period. However, this may not be required for other accounting software programs, which may allow opening balances to be created on the accounts start date. The default opening balance date in this program is the day before the accounts start date; in this case, that is 31/12/2015. This should not be changed.

Therefore if you are instructed in the assessment to enter opening balances at, say, 1 January 2016; on Sage One you should enter the opening balance date as 31 December 2015. Other programs may allow you to enter an opening balance of 1 January 2016.

Note that for any entries made using this option, the other side of the double entry will be posted to a suspense account: A/C 9998 - Opening Balances Control Account. However, since opening balances entered should sum to zero (having the same value of debits and credits), entering all opening balances should result in a zero balance overall on the Opening Balances Control Account.

We will look at entering opening balances for customers and suppliers later in this chapter.

3.5 Tax codes and VAT rates

Other programs may require you to manually set up **tax codes** corresponding to the different VAT rates (eg, zero-rated, standard, reduced and exempt rates). In this program, you do not need to worry about this, as these are automatically set up by Sage.

Occasionally, new VAT rates are introduced or an existing VAT rate percentage is changed. This happened when the UK VAT rate moved from 17.5% to 20% in 2011. In this program, such changes are also automatically updated by Sage. Other programs may require you to manually edit such changes.

At the time of print, the standard VAT rate in the UK is 20%, which is the rate used for this Text. Should there be a change in this rate, the new rate will be automatically updated to the program. However, you will still be able to work through the examples and tasks by selecting the VAT rate as 'Standard'. The only difference will be that the figures for VAT will be calculated using the new rate, rather than 20%, as shown in this Text.

When entering transactions, it is important to use the appropriate VAT rate to ensure the VAT is correctly treated. The VAT rates are summarised below. Note that in the assessment, you do not need to know what the different rates of VAT are used for. You will be told in the assessment if VAT is applicable, and the rate to use.

VAT rate	Used for
Zero-rated	Zero-rated transactions, such as books, magazines and train fares. (Don't confuse this with exempt transactions.)
Standard	Standard rate, currently 20%. Some standard-rated items that catch people out are taxi fares (but only if the taxi driver is VAT registered), restaurant meals, and stationery. You can only reclaim VAT if you have a valid VAT invoice; if not, enter no VAT.
Lower rate	Reduced rate, currently 5% for certain things such as domestic electricity, but this does not normally apply to business expenditure.
Exempt	Exempt transactions such as bank charges and insurance, postage stamps and professional subscriptions.
No VAT*	Transactions not involving VAT, for example wages, charitable donations and internal transfers between accounts (for instance from the bank to the petty cash account). Also used if the supplier is not VAT registered or if you do not have a valid VAT invoice.

* The rate 'No VAT' would also be used for all transactions if your business was not VAT registered. However, in this case study the business is VAT registered.

As mentioned above, you will **not** be expected to know the VAT rates for different goods and services. However, you may find the following list of current VAT rates helpful in real life:

www.gov.uk/rates-of-vat-on-different-goods-and-services

3.6 Trade and non-trade receivables

One thing to note is that Sage One does not make a distinction between trade (customers) and non-trade (also known as 'other') receivables. Anyone to whom you grant credit is simply treated as a customer in Sage One.

Another point to note is that Sage uses old UK GAAP (Generally Accepted Accounting Principles) terminology rather than IFRS (International Financial Reporting Standards) and new UK GAAP terminology and therefore uses terms like 'debtors' rather than 'receivables'. Therefore, the receivables control account in Sage is named 'Trade Debtors'.

Note. From now on, we will use the same terminology as Sage uses (ie old UK GAAP terminology) for the purposes of navigating through Sage. However, please be aware of the equivalent terms used in IFRS and new UK GAAP. A list of these is provided at the front of this Text and it is the IFRS/new UK GAAP terminology that will be used in any questions in tasks in your assessment.

4 Customer and supplier data

Before you can post customer and supplier transactions you will also need to set up accounts in the trade debtors ledger (often referred to as the sales ledger) and the trade creditors ledger (often referred to as the purchase ledger).

Note. Customer and supplier accounts are subsidiary accounts of an overall trade debtors ledger account and trade creditors account respectively. Therefore, transactions entered in all customer accounts will be posted to the **one** trade debtors ledger account in the nominal ledger (and the same treatment applies to supplier accounts and the trade creditors ledger).

Once again, we recommend that you set up all the accounts you need before you start posting any transactions.

In an assessment (and in real life) you will find the details you need on the documents you have to hand: the business's own sales invoices and its suppliers' purchase invoices.

4.1 Customer and supplier codes

You will need to decide what kind of codes to use for the customer and supplier accounts. In Sage One, these codes are entered in the Reference field in the New Supplier/New Customer screens (as we will see in the next section). Note although this field is optional in Sage One, you must create a code, as this is a syllabus requirement. Other programs may refer to the code as a supplier/customer code, or account code, and have a mandatory field for this.

A typical coding system in businesses is to use the first few characters of the supplier/customer name (excluding spaces and punctuation). So, for a customer called 'G.T. Summertown', the code might be GTS. However, this does not allow for customers with similar names. For this reason, many businesses actually introduce numbers into their coding systems. For example, GTS001, GTS002, and so on.

Of course, in your work you would use the coding system prescribed by your organisation. However, in an assessment you will usually be told which code to use. If a task does allow for choice, we recommend an alphanumeric system (a mixture of letters and numbers), as this displays your understanding of the need for understandable but unique codes.

Task 4

Do you think it is possible for a customer and a supplier to have exactly the same code? Explain your answer.

4.2 Entering the account details

We'll now illustrate setting up a supplier account. Please note that the process is identical for customers, apart from the fact that you will be working within the **Customers screens**.

To access the **Suppliers** screen, choose **Contacts > Suppliers**. You are then presented with the following screen.

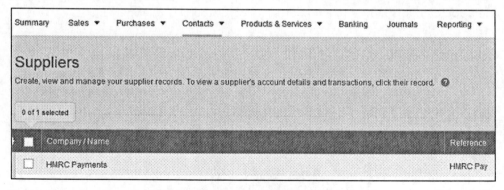

To set up a new account you can click on **New Supplier.**

This brings up the following screen.

Create a new supplier ✕

Business Name*	Company or Person
Contact Name	
Reference	e.g. Account Number

Email	
Mobile	
Telephone	

Account Details   Payment Details   Notes

UK & Ireland ▾

Address 1	
Address 2	
Town / City	
County	
Postcode	
Country	United Kingdom (GB) ▾

VAT Number	
Account Default	5000 - Cost of sales - goods ▾

Save

Enter as many details as you have available. The details you need will usually be found on the supplier invoice. If the invoice shows an email address, for instance, be sure to type it in, even though you may not have email addresses for other suppliers. If you cannot find the relevant field, try moving from tab to tab to find the field you want. Take care with typing, as always. Don't forget to enter the **Supplier Code** referred to in the previous section, in the **Reference** field. When you are happy that everything is correct, click on **Save**. Always remember to click **Save** after entering each supplier.

Task 5

Set up a supplier account based on the following details taken from the heading of an invoice.

McAlistair Supplies Ltd
52 Foram Road
Winnesh
DR3 5TP
Tel: 06112 546772 Mobile: 07700 900009
Email: sales@mcalisupps.co.uk
VAT No. 123456788

Leave the Bank Details section blank and don't change the default Purchase Ledger Account or the Payment Terms settings for now. Remember to **Save** the new account.

You will see that McAlistair Supplies is now listed as a supplier in the main Suppliers screen (**Contacts > Suppliers**).

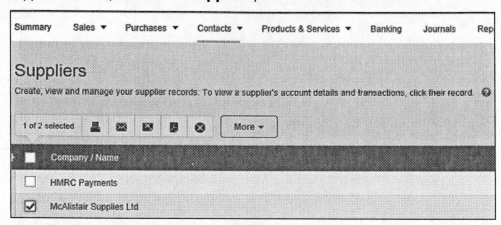

Selecting McAlistair Supplies from the list will bring up the following record.

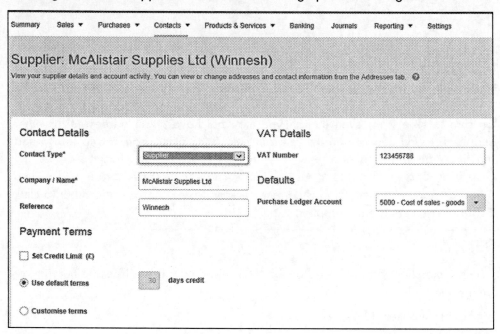

If you make mistake in Task 5 and need to delete the supplier, tick the check-box to the left of the supplier and select the delete icon (circled below) that appears above the **Company Name** heading, as shown in the screen below.

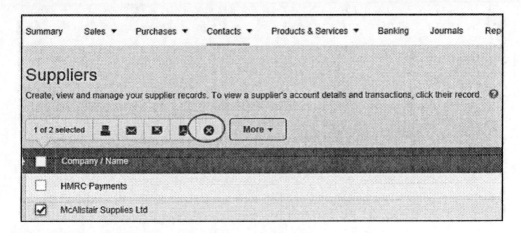

4.3 Entering the opening balance

Earlier in this chapter, we looked at entering an opening balance for a nominal ledger account. The opening balance for the 'Trade creditors' ledger account is made up of the sum of the individual opening supplier balances. The suppliers you are asked to set up in an assessment task may have opening balances. To enter a supplier opening balance, choose the **Settings** tab from the main screen and select **Supplier Opening Balances**. Click on the **New Opening Balance** button and you are presented with the following screen.

The table below explains what to do as you work through each entry field, in the order in which the Tab key will take you through them.

SCREEN ITEM	HOW IT WORKS
Supplier	Select the supplier from the Supplier drop-down list.
Date	As mentioned earlier, when we entered nominal ledger opening balances, Sage One requires the opening balance date to be the **day before** the accounts start date. By default, this field (box) will show this date.
	You should make sure that this is correct; otherwise this means you will not have set up your accounts start date correctly. For this business, the accounts start date is 01/01/2016, therefore the opening balance date should be 31/12/2015.
Type	This program allows you to enter the opening balance as a number of separate entries for individual invoices or credit notes that make up the total balance. This field allows you to specify whether each of these entries is an invoice or credit note. However, this is beyond the scope of this syllabus, as you are only required to enter the total opening balance figure. Therefore, leave this field as Invoice.
Reference	This field would be used to enter the reference number of the invoices or credit notes that make up the total opening balance. However, since this is not applicable, you should enter the initials OB in this field for opening balance.
Details	This field can be left blank.
Total	Enter the total opening balance figure.

Entering customer opening balances is done in the same way, except that you choose **Settings > Customer Opening Balances**.

4.4 Customer and supplier defaults

Ledger account code

In Sage One, when you set up a new customer account, customer invoices you enter will be posted by default to the following account:

DEBIT   Trade debtors account (debit gross amount)

CREDIT   Sales Type A account (credit net amount)

CREDIT   VAT on sales account (credit VAT amount)

For sales, this is probably exactly what you want to happen, unless you are specifically instructed that different types of sales should be posted to different sales accounts in the nominal ledger.

When you set up a new supplier account, the supplier invoices you enter will be posted by default to the following accounts:

DEBIT   VAT on purchases account (debit VAT amount)

DEBIT   Cost of sales account (debit net amount)

CREDIT   Trade creditors account (credit gross amount)

For supplier invoices, however, it would be better to set an appropriate default for the nominal ledger account for each supplier, depending on the type of purchase. For example, you would want to post a stationery supplier's invoices to the stationery account, but an insurance company's invoices to the insurance account.

To change the defaults, just open the supplier record (**Contacts > Suppliers > click on the required supplier**) and click on the box labelled **Purchase Ledger Account**.

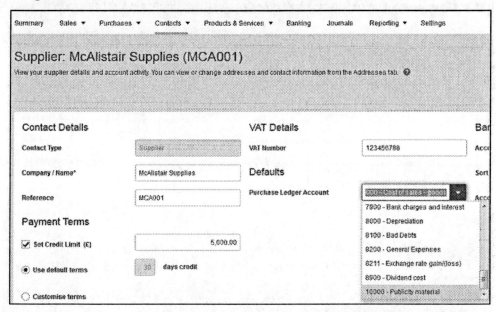

In this box, you can set the nominal ledger expenditure account to which all transactions with this supplier will be posted (unless you specify otherwise when you actually post a transaction). To see a list of all available accounts, click on the arrow  at the right of the box. For example, you may wish to set the default for McAlistair Supplies to Publicity materials.

We could scroll down the list to the Publicity materials account created earlier (account 10000). If you need a new nominal account to post to, you can set one up, as mentioned earlier in Task 2.

Note. If you cannot see the account you created in Task 2, this could be for a couple of reasons. Firstly, go into **Edit Ledger Account** (from **Settings > Chart of accounts**) for the particular account and make sure that you have ticked the option: **Purchases – Invoice / Credit, Product / Supplier defaults** in the **Visibility** section.

If the account still does not appear, try using Sage One in a different internet browser. The main internet browsers available are Internet Explorer, Google Chrome, Mozilla Firefox, and Safari (for Mac users).

Payment terms

The default payment terms (ie how long a supplier gives a customer to pay an invoice) is set to 30 days' credit. If in the assessment you are asked to set up a supplier with payment terms of 30 days, make sure the **Use default terms** option is selected in the Supplier record. If you are asked to set up different payment terms, select the **Customise terms** option and enter the required number of days' credit.

The same process also applies for customers.

Also, a credit limit can also be set for each customer/supplier. Tick the box next to **Set Credit Limit (£)** and enter the amount.

Payment Terms	
☑ Set Credit Limit (£)	5,000.00
◉ Use default terms	30 days credit
◯ Customise terms	

Task 6

Open the McAlistair Supplies Ltd supplier record and set the default nominal code to 10000 - Publicity material; the payment terms, to 30 days; and the credit limit, to £5,000.00.

Remember to **Save** this change.

---

5 Journals

If you are setting up a new business, the first entries you are likely to make will be done via a journal; for example, entering the initial capital introduced to a business.

Journals are also used for non-routine transactions, such as the correction of errors and recording drawings from the business. You will be required to enter journals during your assessment.

To post a journal in Sage, click on the **Journals** tab shown on the home screen and click on **New Journal** to bring up the Journal screen as shown below.

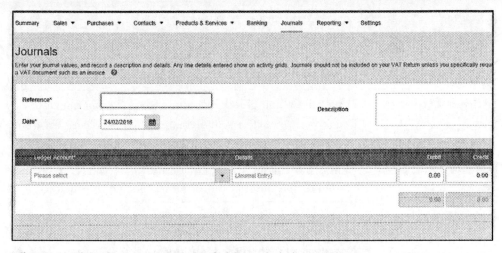

All you need to do is complete the fields and click on **Save**.

Note. Once saved or 'posted' it is not possible to correct a journal and you will need to input another journal to correct any errors, so check carefully before saving.

Let's suppose you want to post the following journal, to enter the initial capital invested in the business.

		£	£
DEBIT	Bank (Current)	2,750.00	
DEBIT	Cash in hand	250.00	
CREDIT	Capital introduced		3,000.00

The table below explains what to do as you work through each entry field in the Journal screen, in the order in which the Tab key will take you through them.

SCREEN ITEM	HOW IT WORKS
Reference	Type in the journal number you are given, if any. Journals should be numbered consecutively, so you may need to check to find out the number of the previous journal. If this is the first ever journal, choose your own coding system and make sure it has room for expansion. For example, 'J001' allows for up to 999 journals in total.
Date	By default, this field (box) will show the PROGRAM DATE, but you should change it to 01/01/16. Clicking the ▦ button will make a little calendar appear to select the date from.

SCREEN ITEM	HOW IT WORKS
Description	Type in the journal narrative, ie the purpose of the journal.
Ledger Account	Enter the nominal ledger code of the account affected, or click the ▾ button to the right of this field to select from a drop-down list.
Details	Enter the details for each journal line. This can be the same as the description, or more specific, if required.
Debit/Credit	Type in the amounts in the correct columns. If it is a round sum, such as £250, there is no need to type in the decimal point and the extra zeros.
Include on VAT Return?	This should be left unchecked, as VAT returns are not covered at this level. Sage One gives you the option of choosing whether you want to include the journal on a VAT return.

It is not possible to post a journal if it does not balance, and the following error message is displayed.

⚠ • The totals of the debits and credits must match.

Task 7

Enter the journal shown earlier in this section (DEBIT Current 2,750, DEBIT Cash 250, CREDIT Capital Introduced 3,000). Date it 01/01/2016 and give a reference of JVI. Enter 'Initial capital' in the description and details fields. Remember to **Save** the journal.

If you run the **Balance Sheet (Reporting > Balance Sheet Report)** at 31/01/2016, you should see that 3,000 is listed against Total Assets and 3,000 listed against Total Equity.

5.1 The importance of dates

By default, Sage One sets the date of transactions to the current date according to your computer, but this may not be the date you want to use, especially if you are sitting an assessment. You can overwrite the default date in each transaction with the required date.

It is vitally important to enter the correct date when you are using a computerised system, even if you are only doing a practice exercise, because the computer uses the date you enter in a variety of ways – to generate reports such as aged debtors reports, to reconcile VAT, and so on.

Furthermore, when viewing reports or lists within Sage, make sure that you have set the date range correctly in the particular report or list – otherwise certain transactions might not show up.

Note. In the assessment, you will be asked to set the **system software date** to a specific date as part of the set-up process. This cannot be done in Sage One, as the system software date defaults to the current date. This does not form part of the assessment and will not affect your ability to perform the assessment as you can overwrite the default date within each function.

6 Entering invoices

You may be feeling that you have been working hard but have not actually accomplished much yet! This is one of the few off-putting things about accounting software: it can take quite a while to set everything up properly before you can really get started.

If you are feeling frustrated, just remember that you only have to set all these details up once. In future, the fact that all the data is available at the touch of a button will save you a vast amount of time, so it really is worth the initial effort.

6.1 Purchase invoices using the Batch Invoice function

Purchase invoices are created by your suppliers, whereas sales invoices are documents you create yourself. That means that it is usually simpler to enter purchase invoices, so we'll deal with those first.

At this level, we are entering basic invoice details. Although there is a function to enter invoices individually (**Purchases > Purchase Invoices > New invoice**), for this exercise we will use the Quick Entry function which allows you to enter basic invoice details for a number of suppliers in batches. Choose **Purchases > Quick Entries > New Quick Entry**) which brings up the **Quick Entry** screen as shown below.

As always, you can use the **Tab** key to move between different parts of the screen.

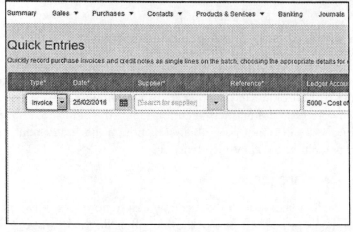

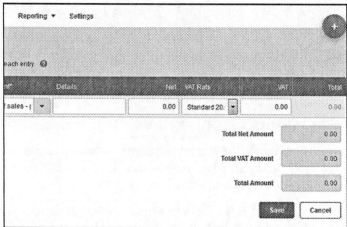

You can enter a number of different invoices from different suppliers on the same screen. You can also enter each line of the same invoice separately, if the invoice is for a variety of items that need to be coded to different nominal accounts. In this case, you should use the same supplier's invoice number in the **Reference** field of each line of the invoice. This will generate a warning message that a similar transaction exists; however, in this instance, this should be ignored and the program will still allow you to save the entries.

The following table explains what to do as you tab through each entry field. Pay particular attention to the **Net**, **VAT rate** and **VAT** fields.

SCREEN ITEM	HOW IT WORKS
Type	Select either Invoice to enter an invoice, or Cr Note to enter a credit note from the drop-down list (click on the ☑ button).
Date	The program date will be entered by default, but you can change this if you wish. Clicking the ☐ button will make a little calendar appear.
Supplier	Select the supplier account from the drop-down list (click on the ☑ button).
Reference	Type in the supplier's invoice number.
Ledger Account	This will show the default ledger expenditure account code associated with this supplier. If you need to change it, click on the ☑ button to see a list of nominal ledger accounts.
Details	Type in a brief but clear description of the item and be sure that your description will be understood by someone other than you. Usually, you will just need to copy the description on the supplier's invoice.
Net	Enter the net amount of the invoice, ie excluding VAT. If the invoice has several lines, you can enter each line separately but you should use the same reference for each line.
	If, in the assessment, you are only given the gross amount, (ie, the amount including VAT), the net amount is equal to the gross amount ÷ (1 + VAT rate). For example, £10 gross = 10 ÷ (1.20) = £8.33 net (where the VAT rate = 20%).
VAT Rate	Select the appropriate rate for the item (see 'Tax codes and VAT rates' section earlier). If this field does not appear, check that you have set up your VAT scheme correctly by choosing **Settings > Financial Year & VAT**.
VAT	This item will be calculated automatically, depending on the VAT rate selected. Check that it agrees with the VAT shown on the actual invoice. You can overtype the automatic amount, if necessary.

When you have entered all the invoice details, you post them simply by clicking on **Save**. This will post **all** the required accounting entries to the ledgers.

Task 8

Post an invoice from McAlistair Supplies dated 6 January 2016 for 2,000 sheets of A4 paper (net price: £20.35, ledger account: Publicity material) and a box of 100 blue promotional biros (gross price: £10.00, ledger account: Office costs). The invoice number is PG45783 and VAT is applicable on each transaction at the standard rate. **Save** and **Close**.

Write down the total amount of VAT.

£	

6.2 Nominal Activity Report

The first time you do this you will probably not quite believe that double entry to all the ledgers can be so easy. To check that the purchase invoice has been posted you can view the transaction in individual nominal ledger accounts. To check the nominal ledger, choose **Reporting > Nominal Activity**. This brings up a list of each ledger account. Select a date range in the **From** and **To** boxes that is around the transaction date of the invoice, eg 01/01/2016 to 31/01/2016.

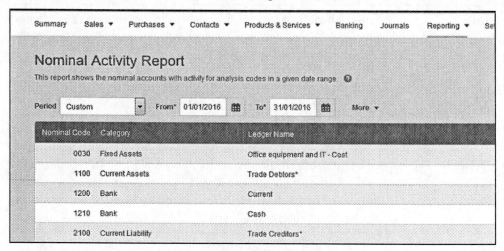

Depending on which type of transaction you posted (ie a customer invoice or supplier invoice) you should then click on either 1100 - Trade Debtors (the debtors ledger control account) or 2100 - Trade Creditors (the creditors ledger control account).

This brings up the **Detailed Nominal Activity** screen for the Trade Creditors account. You will see that the transaction has been correctly posted to the Trade Creditors Account, as shown in the screens below.

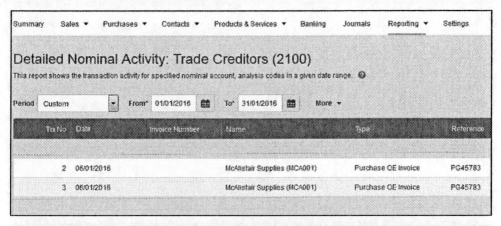

What about the other accounts of the double entry that make up the full transaction? For the invoice from McAlistair Supplies, the double entry should be as follows:

DEBIT   VAT on purchases account (debit VAT amount)

DEBIT   Publicity Material (debit net amount)

DEBIT   Office costs (debit net amount)

CREDIT   Trade Creditors (credit gross amount)

You can also check that the transaction has been correctly posted to the Publicity Material account (A/C code 10000), the Office Costs account (A/C code 7500) and the VAT on purchases account (A/C code 2201) by running the Nominal Activity report as described above.

Furthermore, to check that the correct amounts have also been posted to the subsidiary account (ie the individual supplier account within the overall Trade Creditors account), open the supplier record (**Contacts > Suppliers > Click on McAlistair Supplies Ltd**) and click on the **Activity** tab.

This shows a list of all transactions that have been made to the supplier account at the bottom of the screen for a particular date range. If no transactions appear, you may need to change the date range in the **From** and **To** boxes. This list can also

be refined by transaction type and outstanding amounts by clicking on the **Filters** button.

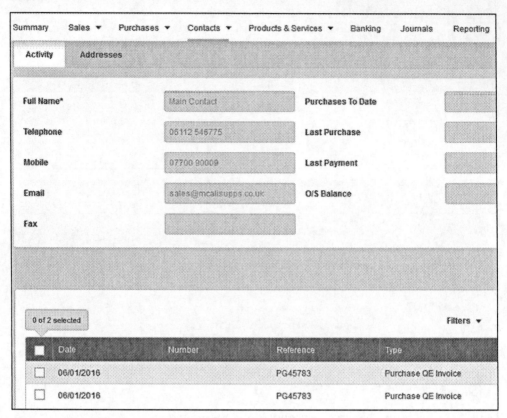

Finally, if you just want a quick look at the transactions you have posted, you can run the **Audit trail**. This shows a list of transactions that have been posted. Choose **Reporting > Audit Trail.** This shows a summary audit trail. Click on **Detailed** to see the detailed version.

Don't forget to ensure the date range is sufficient to include the transactions by selecting **Custom** from the drop-down list in the **Period** field, and specifying the date range in the **From Date** and **To Date** fields. This report can also be exported to a PDF or CSV file by clicking on the **Export** button.

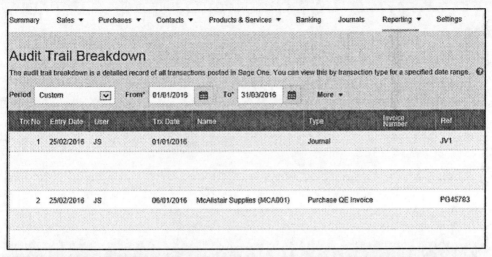

Ref	Ledger Account	Debit	Credit
JV1	Cash (1210)	250.00	0.00
	Capital introduced (3200)	0.00	3,000.00
	Current (1200)	2,750.00	0.00
PG45783	Publicity material (10000)	20.35	0.00
	VAT on Purchases (2201)	4.07	0.00
	Trade Creditors (2100)	0.00	24.42

6.3 Sales invoices – if no invoice is produced

Some businesses create sales invoices using a different system from their accounting software – for example, using word processing software such as Word. The invoices are then entered into the computerised accounting software.

If that is the case, then sales invoices are entered in exactly the same way as purchase invoices. To do this, click on **Sales** then **Quick Entries** and enter the invoices in a batch, in a similar way as you did for the purchase invoice above.

6.4 Sales invoices – if the program creates the invoice

In Sage One, you can produce printable invoices. If you wanted to do this, you could do so by clicking on **Sales > Sales Invoices** and then the **New Invoice** button. The invoice details can then be entered, saved and an invoice printed.

However, in the assessment you will be given a list of invoices or sample invoices to enter. Therefore, you should only enter invoices using the Quick Entry method described earlier, rather than creating an invoice.

Task 9

(1) Set up two more **suppliers** with the following details.

Widgets Unlimited Ltd
123 High Road
London
W23 2RG
020 8234 2345

Office Products Ltd
321 Low Road
London
E32 2GR
020 8432 5432

(2) Process the purchase of:

(a) 10 widgets (Cost of sales - materials) from Widgets Unlimited Ltd for a total net cost of £80. Invoice number WU4474, dated 8 January 2016.

(b) A computer (Office equipment and IT - Cost*) from Office Products Ltd for a net cost of £800. Invoice OP1231, dated 10 January 2016.

Both purchases attract VAT at the standard rate.

* If the 'Office equipment and IT – Cost' account does not appear in the list of ledger accounts to select from, this means that it is not visible within this particular function of the program. To make it visible choose **Settings > Chart of Accounts > Click on the Office equipment and IT – Cost account**. This brings up the **Edit Ledger Account** screen. To make this account visible in the Purchases function, make sure there is a tick in the check box next to the **Purchases – Invoice/Credit, Product/Supplier defaults** option in the **Visibility** section of this screen as shown below.

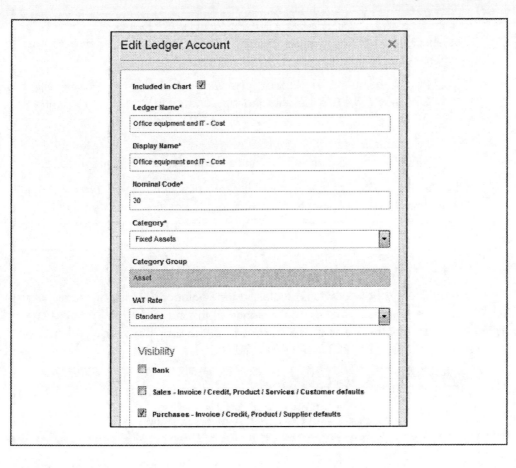

Task 10

(1)   Set up a new **customer** with the following details.

Alexander Ltd
501 Dart Road
Leeds
LS12 6TC
0113 245 3241
info@alexander.co.uk

30 days' credit (payment due days)
All other fields can be left blank.

(2)   Set up a new nominal code called 'Sales Type B'.

(3) Post the following two invoices (remember, you have to use **Save** to post them) to this customer:

   (a) Invoice number 001: Product: 10 widgets at a selling price (net) of £20 each. VAT to be charged at standard rate. Date: 15 January 2016.

   (b) Invoice number 002: Service: Advice on widgets, at a fee of £50 (net). VAT to be charged at standard rate. Date: 25 January 2016.

(4) Change the names of the nominal ledger accounts 'Sales Type A' and 'Sales Type B' as necessary to accommodate the different sales types in (3).

Task 11

As you should know from previous studies, a trial balance is a list of balances of all the ledger accounts. Preview a trial balance at this stage. Select **Reporting > Trial Balance**, set the **Period** as **Custom** from the drop-down list, and specify the date range as 01/01/2016 to 31/01/2016.

		Debit	Credit
0030	Office equipment and IT - Cost	800.00	
1100	Trade Debtors	300.00	
1200	Current	2,750.00	
1210	Cash	250.00	
2100	Trade Creditors		1,090.42
2200	VAT on Sales		50.00
2201	VAT on Purchases	181.74	
3200	Capital introduced		3,000.00
4000	Sales - products		200.00
5010	Cost of sales - materials	80.00	
7500	Office costs	8.33	
10000	Publicity material	20.35	
10001	Sales - services		50.00
	TOTAL	£4,390.42	£4,390.42

6.5 Credit notes

If a supplier issues a credit note, for example to account for a return of goods, or to correct an error on their part, a standalone credit note should be entered. This is posted in exactly the same way as a supplier invoice, in the Quick Entries screen, except that you select **Cr Note** instead of **Invoice** in the **Type** field.

Customer credit notes can be posted in this way too.

If you have posted a supplier invoice with errors you made yourself and want to correct it, although the program allows you to amend the original invoice, we recommend that you correct it with a standalone credit note. This provides a clearer audit trail.

7 Help!

7.1 Help in Sage

If ever you are unsure about how to perform a task in Sage, take a look on the online **Help page**. This is accessed by pressing the 🔘 button.

We recommend you explore the options shown below in the Help page. There are a number of useful guides on how to perform common tasks.

To search for help on a specific topic, enter the topic into the search bar and click on the magnifying glass icon in the right of the bar.

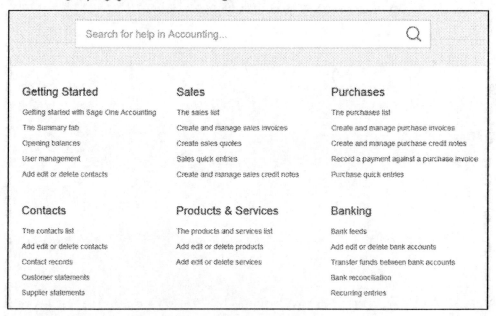

Experiment with this; the ability to find out how to do something yourself could come in handy in your work and in your assessment.

7.2 Help from your manager and others

Whenever you are unsure about what to do, or are faced with an error message you are unsure about, the golden rule is to **ask for help or advice**.

Don't ignore error messages. If possible, have your manager or someone more senior look at the message immediately and advise you on what action to take. If you need to provide details for someone if they can't get to your screen to view it, take a screenshot for them.

Chapter overview

- Accounting software programs range from simple bookkeeping tools to more complex software. Sage's products are among the most popular software programs in the UK.

- Assessments may involve setting up new customer and supplier accounts, posting journals, invoices, payments and receipts, and producing reports or other types of output.

- New nominal ledger accounts can be set up using the accounting software program's chart of accounts.

- VAT is dealt with by assigning the correct VAT rate to a transaction.

- New customer and supplier accounts should be given consistent and meaningful codes.

- Familiarise yourself with the Help feature; it could come in handy both in your work and in your assessment.

- Never ignore error messages – ask for help or advice from your manager.

Keywords

- **Activity:** the transactions that have occurred within an account
- **Chart of accounts:** a template that sets out the nominal ledger accounts and how they are organised into different categories
- **Customer:** a person or organisation that buys products or services from your organisation
- **Customer record:** the details relating to the customer account, for example name and address, contact details and credit terms
- **Defaults:** the entries that the accounting software program expects to normally be made in a particular field
- **Field:** a box on screen in which you enter data or select from a list (similar to a spreadsheet cell)
- **General ledger:** the ledger containing the income statement (profit and loss) and statement of financial position (balance sheet) accounts
- **Ledger accounts:** accounts in which each transaction is recorded
- **Nominal ledger:** another term for General Ledger; Sage uses this term for the ledger containing the income statement (profit or loss) and statement of financial position (balance sheet) accounts
- **Supplier:** a person or organisation that your organisation buys products or services from
- **Supplier record:** the details relating to the supplier account, for example name and address, contact details and credit terms
- **Trade creditors ledger:** the collection of supplier accounts, also known as the purchase ledger
- **Trade debtors ledger:** the collection of customer accounts, also known as the sales ledger
- **VAT rate:** the percentage rate of Value Added Tax on a transaction

Test your learning

1   What is a 'field' in an accounting software program?

2   What do you understand by the term 'default'?

3   What is a chart of accounts?

4   What must be set up before a supplier invoice can be posted?

5   How would a supplier invoice be assigned to the correct nominal ledger account?

6   If you attempt to post a journal that does not balance, the difference will be posted to a suspense account. True or false? Explain your answer.

7   If a purchase invoice has five separate lines, should these be posted individually or is it sufficient just to post the invoice totals?

Sage One – part 2

4

Chapter coverage

The topics covered in this chapter follow on from where you should have reached in Chapter 3.

The subjects covered in this chapter are:

- Payments and receipts
- Bank reconciliations
- Reports and other types of output
- Error correction
- Irrecoverable debts
- Month-end procedures

1 Payments and receipts

Your assessment may include details of payments and receipts to enter into the accounts. These could comprise cash, cheques and automated payments.

You need to be able to distinguish between cheques that you have sent to **suppliers** and cheques received from **customers**. If it is a cheque that you have paid out to a SUPPLIER you may only be shown the cheque stub (that's all you would have in practice, after all), such as illustrated below.

Date ....

Payee ....

....

....

....

£ ....

000001

If it is a cheque that you have received from a customer, you may be shown the cheque itself.

Lloyds TSB   **30-92-10**

Benham Branch   Date _____

Pay _____

_____

_____

FOR WHITEHILL SUPERSTORES

You can tell that this is a receipt because the name below the signature (here, Whitehill Superstores) will be the name of one of your customers.

In the assessment, you could also be given details of an electronic payment or receipt, for example, a BACS remittance advice detailing a receipt from a customer.

Alternatively, you may be shown a paying-in slip that may include receipts from several different customers.

Cheques etc.			Brought forward £				£50		
							£20		
							£10		
							£5		
							£2		
							£1		
							50p		
							20p		
							Silver		
			Whitehill	1468	75		Bronze		
			Superstores				Total Cash		
							Cardnet	3818	75
			G T				Cheques		
			Summerfield	2350	00		etc.		
Carried forward £			Carried forward £	3818	75	Total £		3818	75
Date 23/01/2016		500001	FOR SFE MERCHANDISING			06325143			

1.1 Supplier payments

When you pay a supplier, it is important to allocate your payment to invoices shown as outstanding in the purchase ledger. Sage makes this very easy.

There are a number of different payment allocations that can occur in both the sales and purchase ledger. Usually, you will pay most invoices in full or take a credit note in full; however, there may be reasons why an invoice may only be partially paid, due to disputes or cash flow problems. These are unsurprisingly known as 'part payments'. Occasionally, you may not be able to allocate a payment or receipt because it is for an invoice not on the system or the amount does not match with your ledger. In these cases, the payment is recorded against the correct account but not to any particular invoice or credit note and these are known as 'payments on account'.

Discounts can be allowed on payments received from customers (or received on payments made to suppliers), and a discount field is available to make a note of these amounts.

Payments allocated to invoices

To post a payment to a supplier, click on **Banking** on the main screen and then click on the required bank account. Then select **New Entry > Purchase/Payment > Supplier Payment**.

You are presented with the Supplier Payment screen. If you enter McAlistair Supplies Ltd in the **Supplier** field, the bottom half of the screen shows details of the outstanding invoices, as shown below.

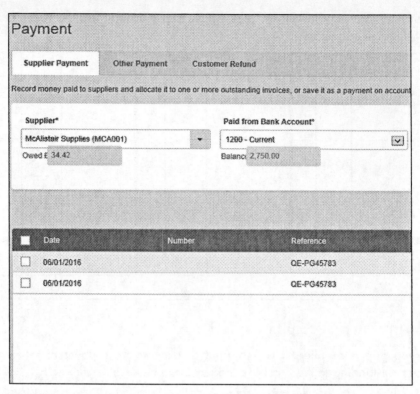

The following table explains the quickest way to post a payment and allocate it to supplier invoices. Press **Tab** to move from one field to the next.

SCREEN ITEM	HOW IT WORKS
Supplier	Enter the supplier name or supplier code. Entering the first few characters will bring up a list of suppliers which you can select from.
Paid from Bank Account	Select the bank account from which the payment was made from the drop-down list.
Date Paid	Enter the date the payment was made. The program date will be entered by default, but you can change this by clicking on the ▦ calendar button.
Reference	This is an optional field but can be used to enter a reference to identify the transaction, eg a cheque number. If you are making a payment directly from the bank account such as a BACS payment, you can put the BACS reference in this field. This will help with bank reconciliations.
Amount Paid	Though it might seem odd, leave this at 0.00 when paying an invoice in full, as it will automatically be filled in when you select the invoice. Select the required invoice for payment by ticking the check box next to it.

■	Date	Number	Reference
☑	06/01/2016		QE-PG45783
☐	06/01/2016		QE-PG45783

Using this method, the **Amount Paid** field updates each time you select an invoice.

	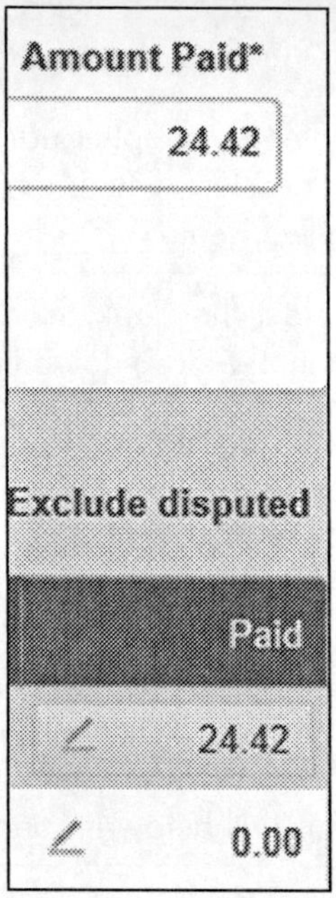
	Amount Paid* 24.42 Exclude disputed Paid ∠ 24.42 ∠ 0.00
Discount	Tab past this if there is no discount. However, if you do need to process a discount, this brings up a screen where you should enter the discounted amount in the **Amount to pay** field and the program will calculate the discount. Then click **Apply**.
Save	This saves to all the ledgers.
Owed	This shows the total outstanding balance.
Balance	This shows the current bank balance for the selected bank account.

You don't need to pay all the outstanding invoices if you don't want to. You can just click on **Save** when you've paid the ones you want.

When you click on Save, this will post the transaction to the relevant accounts. Make sure you have all the correct information before you save.

This is the quickest way of posting a payment in ordinary circumstances.

Part payments

There may be times when you don't want to pay invoices in full. For instance, you may decide to pay the supplier in the illustration above only £20.00 for the selected invoice, perhaps because of some problem with the items supplied. In that case, proceed as follows.

SCREEN ITEM	HOW IT WORKS
Supplier	As before
Date Paid	As before
Ref	As before
Amount Paid	Though it might seem odd, leave this at 0.00
Paid	Click in this field and the following screen comes up Part Pay ✕ Enter the amount you want to pay: Reference Outstanding 24.42 Amount to pay 20.00 Discount 0.00 New outstanding amount 4.42 Apply Cancel
Amount to pay	Type in the amount you want to pay
Discount	Tab past this
Apply	This applies the payment to the main payment screen

Applying a credit note to a payment

A further possibility is that there will be a credit note on the account as well as invoices. When you reach the credit note line in the list of outstanding items in the bottom half of the screen, click the check box and the **Amount Paid** field will be reduced by the credit note amount.

Unallocated payments (payment on account)

There may be times when you need to record a supplier payment but are unable to allocate it to an invoice, either partially or wholly.

For instance, you may decide to pay the supplier in the illustration above only £10.00 but not apply this yet to an invoice(s). In that case, proceed as follows.

SCREEN ITEM	HOW IT WORKS
Supplier	As before
Date Paid	As before
Ref	As before
Amount Paid	Enter the amount paid

Click on **Save** and a warning screen comes up asking you to confirm that you want to save the unallocated payment on account. Click **Yes**.

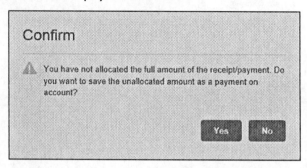

Such payments should be allocated as soon as the relevant information or invoice is available.

Note that VAT is not accounted for on supplier payments. VAT will have already been accounted for when the supplier invoice was posted. Other types of payment may require VAT to be accounted for when the payment entry is made (see 'Other payments and receipts' below).

Task 1

Post a payment on 31/01/16 made with a reference of 158002 to McAlistair Supplies Ltd for the total of invoice PG45783. Remember to click **Save** to effect the posting.

When you post a supplier payment, you also have the option of generating a remittance advice, to be sent to the supplier to inform them of the invoices your business is paying. To do this, you use the **Print Remittance** button available by clicking the down arrow next to the **Save** button. Note that this will save the payment and generate the remittance in one action. You may be asked to generate a remittance during your assessment.

An example is given in the screenshot that follows. You can try this for yourself and generate a remittance.

To recall the payment made in Task 1, click on **Banking,** select **Current,** and then click on the **Activity** tab further down the screen. If you can't see the payment, make sure the **From** and **To** dates are sufficient to include the date of the payment. You can then select the payment from the list.

When you click on **Print Remittance**, this generates the remittance in a new window in your internet browser, similar to that shown below. This can then be saved to your computer as a PDF from your internet browser menu.

SFE Merchandising

SFE Merchandising
14b Hapgood House Dagenham Avenue Benham DR6 8LV

Telephone: VAT Number
07796786718   GB 524376451

McAlistair Supplies (MCA001)

52 Foram Road Winnesh DR3 5TP

Remittance Advice

Reference: 158002   Date Paid: 31/01/2016   Amount Paid: 34.42

Ref	Number	Date	Total Amount	Amount Paid
PG45783		06/01/2016	24.42	24.42
PG45783		06/01/2016	10.00	10.00
			Total Paid:	34.42

1.2 Customer receipts

When you receive money from your customers, it is important to allocate your payment to invoices shown as outstanding.

To record a receipt from an account customer, click on **Banking** on the main menu and then click on the required bank. Then select **New Entry > Sale/Receipt > Customer Receipt**.

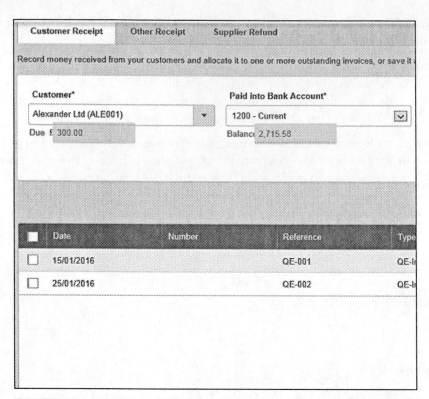

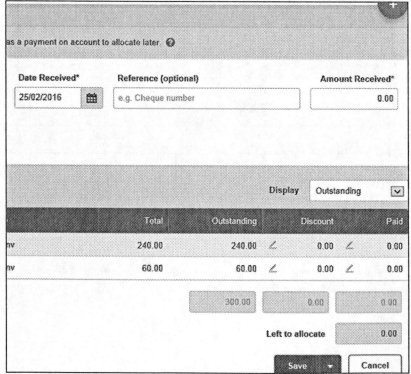

Although this screen looks slightly different from the payment one, it works in exactly the same way, and we recommend that you use it in exactly the same way – in other words, tick the invoices that you have received payment for (which automatically updates the **Amount Received** field), and click on **Save**. If you have unallocated receipts or partial receipts, this works in the same way as described in the 'Supplier payments' section above.

If you are paying in cash and cheques to the bank, one important point to remember when posting receipts is that you should use the paying-in slip number (if you have it) for the **Reference**. This makes it much easier to complete bank reconciliations, because typically, several cheques will be paid in on a single paying-in slip and the bank statement will only show the total, not the individual amounts. If you receive payment electronically, you should use the reference that appears on your bank statement for the receipt, or on the remittance advice from the customer.

Task 2

Post a receipt from Alexander Ltd for £240. This was paid in using paying-in slip 500001 dated 31 January 2016. You should allocate this against Invoice 001. Remember to click **Save** to effect the posting.

1.3 Other payments and receipts (non-credit transactions)

Some payments and receipts do not need to be allocated to customers or suppliers (ie non-credit transactions). Examples include payments like wages and receipts such as cash sales.

If your assessment includes transactions like this, you should post them by clicking the **Banking** tab on the main screen and then clicking on the required bank account.

Then select **New Entry > Sale/Receipt > Other Receipt,** for a receipt (or **New Entry > Purchase/Payment > Other Payment,** for a payment).

You are presented with the **Other Receipt** screen similar to that shown below.

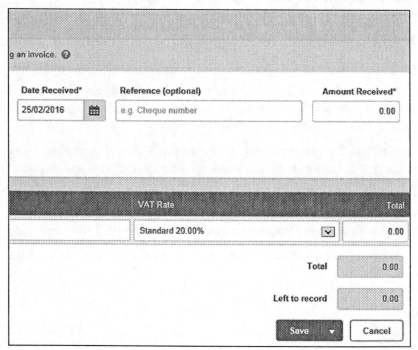

The main differences here to the customer receipt screen earlier are that you enter the amount of the receipt directly in the **Amount Received** field, and that you select the **Ledger Account** where the other side of the double entry for this transaction will be posted to. Note that you can split the receipt into different transactions by entering the details in a new line.

VAT on other payments and receipts

Another difference to the customer receipt screen is that you have to specify the VAT treatment of the transaction. VAT is not accounted for on a receipt of payment of a sales invoice from a credit customer (a customer receipt). This is because VAT will already have been accounted for when the sales invoice was posted.

However, for most 'other receipts,' including cash sales[1], the receipt and related sales transaction are recorded in this one transaction. Therefore you must account for any VAT applicable at this stage. Refer to the Tax Codes and VAT rates section in Chapter 3 for the VAT rates to use.

If the receipt or payment includes VAT, in this program, you should enter the **gross amount** of the receipt or payment. The program then automatically calculates the VAT, and posts it to the correct VAT ledger account when you save the entry.

> (1)   The term 'cash sale' actually refers to a sale where the sale and receipt of payment occur at the same time. For example, a supermarket sells goods to customers who pay for them immediately – these are cash sales. The payment does not necessarily have to be in cash. Payment can also be by cheque, credit or debit card. Cash sales differ to 'credit sales' in that credit sales allow the customer to pay for the goods or services at a later date (typically 30 days later). Another example of cash sales is sales made online over the internet.

'Other payments' and 'other receipts' that don't involve sales or purchases (eg, wages, loans etc) do not attract VAT, and the VAT code to use in these cases is 'No VAT'.

Example of a non-credit transaction

The screen that follows shows an example of how online cash sales might be posted to the accounts using the method described above (don't carry out the transaction). Use the **Ledger Account** drop-down to find which ledger account to use (create a new one if there is not already an appropriate account, using the method described in Task 2 in Chapter 3 – remember to ensure the correct check-boxes are ticked in the Visibility section when creating the account to ensure that the account appears).

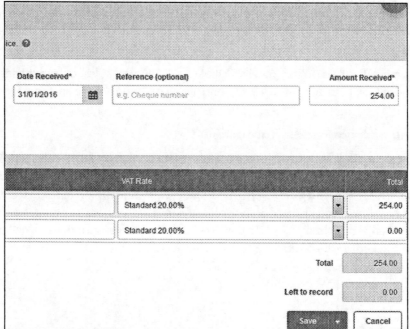

The screen for posting 'other payments' such as wages is exactly the same but instead of using the Other Receipts screen, you access the payments screen through **Other Payments**.

1.4 Direct debits and standing orders (recurring payments)

Many businesses have regular recurring payments, such as rent and rates, set up by standing order or direct debit. It can be easy to forget to post these – especially as some may be monthly, some quarterly and so on. Sage One makes it easy to automate this process.

The process is described as follows but don't carry this out until Tasks 3 and 4. Firstly, you need to create and save the first payment using the 'Other Payments' function, as described above. Enter the reference as 'DD' if it is a direct debit, or 'STO' if it is a standing order. This will help identify the transaction when doing the bank reconciliation.

Then choose **Banking** and click on the bank account where the initial payment was created.

Go to the **Activity** screen and you will see the payment. Make sure that the date range is sufficient to include the payment by entering dates in the **From** and **To** fields.

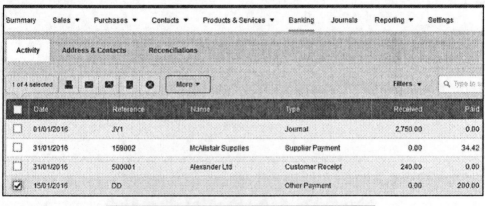

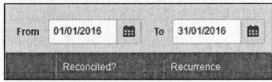

Click on the payment which brings up the details of the payment.

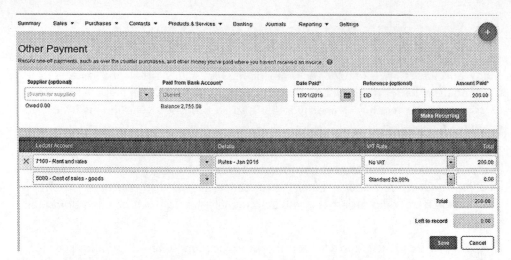

On this screen, click on the **Make Recurring** button; this will bring up a screen like the one that follows. It allows you to specify the frequency and end date of the recurring payment. Clicking on **Save** will activate the recurring payment. The program will then automatically post each payment on the specified date each month.

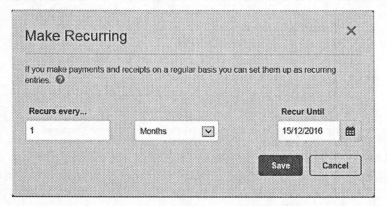

The recurring payment will be identifiable on the **Activity** screen within the banking screen with a 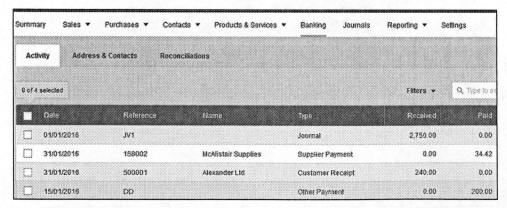 button next to it under the **Recurrence** heading.

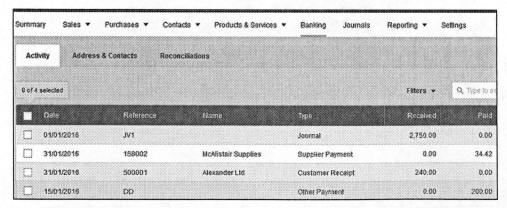

Paid	Cleared	Reconciled?	Recurrence
0.00			
34.42			
0.00			
200.00			⇄

To view the details of the recurrence, click on the recurring payment shown in the **Activity** screen above, which brings up a screen showing the details of the payment. Then click on the **Edit Recurring** button in this screen.

This brings up the following screen which shows the details of the recurrence.

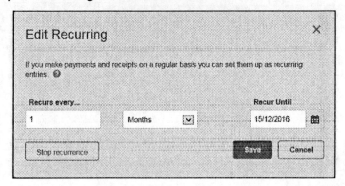

The example above shows how the details of a regular monthly payment for rates could be entered. Note that you may be asked to take screenshots of the screens shown above during the assessment as evidence of you setting up a recurring entry.

Note. In the assessment, as well as being asked to set up a recurring payment, you may be asked to process the first payment. Creating and posting the first payment, as described above, will cover the requirement of processing the first payment.

Task 3

Post the first rates payment shown in the example above, ie £200 for **January 2016 only**, starting on 15 January 2016.

Task 4

Enter and save the recurring rates payment details shown in the example above, ie £200 per month for a further 11 months after the initial payment.

1.5 Petty cash

Petty cash transactions are posted in exactly the same way as non-credit bank payment and receipts (you should refer to the 'Other payments and receipts' section earlier), except that you use the petty cash ('Cash') bank account rather than the bank current account. As with non-credit payments and receipts, VAT is accounted for when entering the transaction for payment or receipt. Therefore, take care to use the correct VAT rate.

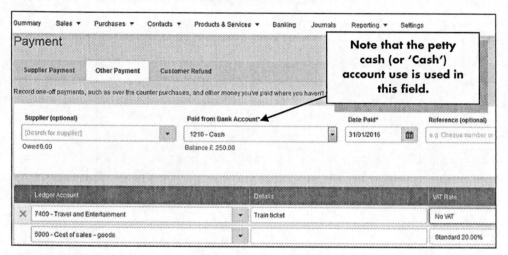

2 Bank reconciliations

As you should know from previous studies a bank reconciliation is a comparison between the bank balance recorded in the accounts and the balance on the bank statement. The differences are called reconciling items and are usually payments and receipts that have not yet cleared the bank account.

To access the bank reconciliation screens, you need to click on **Banking** and then click on the account you want to reconcile. In Sage, the default bank current account is account 1200 – Current. Select this and then click on the arrow next to the **Connect to Bank** button, and select **Reconcile**.

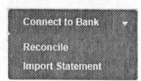

This brings up the **Bank Reconciliation** screen. The first part of this screen gives you the opportunity to enter the bank statement date and balance:

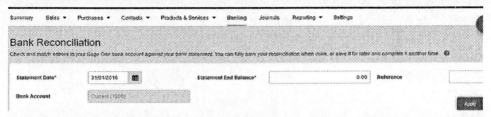

Say that the closing bank statement balance is £2,790.00. That figure would be entered in the **Statement End Balance** box. If the statement is dated 31/01/2016 that can be entered in the **Statement Date** box. The reference field is optional but it is advisable to enter a reference such as the bank statement page number or the date of the reconciliation. Once you have entered these, click **Apply** to start reconciling.

In the main part of the **Bank Reconciliation** screen you will see that initially, all amounts are unmatched, as they do not have a tick in the **'Reconciled'** column:

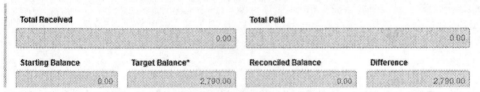

This is also evident as the **Reconciled Balance** box at the bottom shows 0.00:

Total Received		Total Paid	
	0.00		0.00

Starting Balance	Target Balance*	Reconciled Balance	Difference
0.00	2,790.00	0.00	2,790.00

However, by looking at the bank statement, some of these transactions will be found to appear there. We can match these items. Say that the initial journal of £2,750 into the bank account, the rates payment of £200 and the receipt of £240 from Alexander Ltd are also on the bank statement. These can be selected and matched by ticking the check box next to the transaction in the **Reconciled?** column (note that if you accidentally match the wrong entry, then you can untick these).

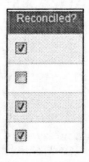

The bottom part of the **Bank Reconciliation** screen will then look as follows:

Total Received		Total Paid	
	2,990.00		200.00

Starting Balance	Target Balance*	Reconciled Balance	Difference
0.00	2,790.00	2,790.00	0.00

Reconciliation has been achieved! The target balance, ie Statement End Balance = Reconciled Balance. The unmatched item of £34.42 explains the difference between the statement balance of £2,790.00 and the Sage bank current account ledger balance of £2,755.58 at 31 January 2016.

Click on the **Finish** button to complete the bank reconciliation. If you have not finished, you can save the reconciliation for later by clicking on the **Save for later** button.

Finish ▼
Save for later

When you go back into the **Bank Reconciliation** screen, the incomplete reconciliation will be there. If you need to start again, you can select **Unreconcile all entries** from the **Interest and Charges** drop-down menu.

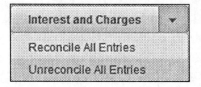

Interest and Charges ▼
Reconcile All Entries
Unreconcile All Entries

Task 5

Carry out the bank reconciliation explained in this section, as at 31 January 2016, assuming that the closing bank statement balance is £2,790.

Although we look at reports in detail later in the chapter, at this stage it is worth pointing out that you can generate a bank reconciliation report (a bank reconciliation statement) from the **Bank Reconciliation** screen.

You can see completed reconciliations by choosing **Banking,** clicking on required bank account, selecting the **Reconciliations** tab in the bottom half of the screen, and selecting a bank reconciliation.

Clicking on **Print** generates the bank reconciliation report in a new window in your internet browser, similar to that shown below. This can be saved to your computer as a PDF file from your internet browser menu.

SFE Merchandising

SFE Merchandising
14b Hapgood House , Dagenham Avenue, Benham, DR6 8LV,
United Kingdom

Telephone: VAT Number
07796786718   GB 524376451

Bank Account	Current (1200)			Statement Date	31/01/2016
Reference				Reconciled By	John See

Date	Reference	Name	Category	Paid	Received
01/01/2016	JV1		Journal	0.00	2,750.00
31/01/2016	500001	Alexander Ltd	Customer Receipt	0.00	240.00
15/01/2016	DD		Other Payment	200.00	0.00

Total Received	2,990.00
Total Paid	200.00
Starting Balance	0.00
Statement End Balance	2,790.00
Reconciled Balance	2,790.00
Difference	0.00

2.1 Adjustments for additional items on the bank statement

Even if you have posted all your transactions correctly, there is a good chance that there will still be items on the bank statement that you have not included in the accounts. Bank charges and interest are common examples.

Unrecorded bank transactions such as bank charges and interest paid or received should be entered using the method described in the **Other payments and receipts** section. Make sure you select the appropriate VAT rate and the appropriate nominal ledger code: 7900 - Bank charges and interest.

3 Reports and other types of output

3.1 The importance of reports generated by the accounting systems

One of the most important features of an accounting system such as Sage One is its ability to provide a range of useful accounting information very quickly. If transactions are entered correctly in the first instance, then accurate summaries or detailed analysis should be available at the click of a button.

To give a simple example of the use of a report by finance staff: **the aged debtors report** can be generated from Sage One (as we will see later) and this will show how old each customer balance is. This will alert staff in charge of credit control to those accounts that are overdue and need chasing for payment, without them having to look back at the invoice dates.

The majority of the reports we will look at are usually produced periodically and used to check on the accuracy of the records.

We will look at generating a **nominal activity report**, which details all the transactions in a period in each account. A quick review of this report can help to identify errors, for example, transactions posted to the wrong account. The trial balance generated by the accounting system may also highlight errors, for example, if a suspense account has been set up and not yet been cleared.

We looked at bank reconciliations earlier and checking the related report against the bank statements is an important procedure that should be carried out regularly.

The various reports can also be used to gain an overview of different financial areas and as a tool when dealing with customers and suppliers. Areas focused on might include identifying and dealing with overdue customer invoices (aged debtors), seeing which suppliers are due for payment (aged creditors) and establishing the cash available to the business to meet its commitments (bank related reports).

3.2 Generating reports

When you have finished entering transactions, the final task in your assessment will be to generate some reports.

Sage One offers you a large number of different standard reports. Although the pre-prepared reports that are available in Sage don't all have names that you will immediately recognise from your knowledge of manual accounting systems, rest assured that everything you are likely to be asked to produce in an assessment can easily be found.

One or two reports, such as customer statements, have their own buttons within the functions they relate to but, in general, to generate most other reports, click on **Reporting** and you are presented with a suite of reports.

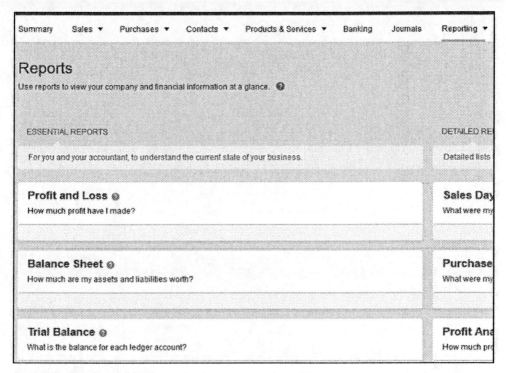

Aged Debtors Report

Click on **Aged Debtors** to generate a summary aged debtors report. Clicking on calendar icon next to the **To** field allows you to select the date you want to report the aged debtors up to.

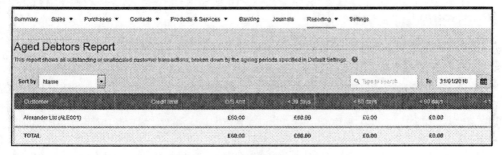

To view a detailed report, click on the **Detailed** button.

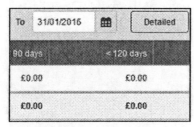

This brings up the detailed aged debtors report:

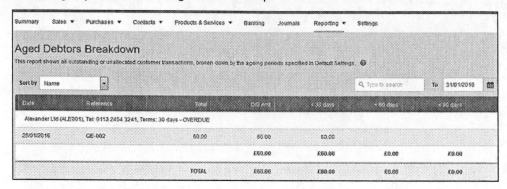

The next step is to select the type of output you require.

Use the **Export** button to export the report as a PDF file and save it to your computer. Please refer to the 'Exporting to PDF file' section in Chapter 3 for details on how to do this.

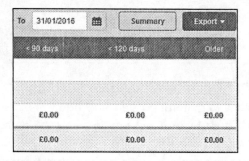

Nominal Activity Report

Another key report is the Nominal Activity Report. This details all the transactions in a period for each account.

To run this report, choose **Reporting > Nominal** Activity. You are initially presented with a screen similar to that shown below which shows a summary of the debits and credits posted to each nominal ledger account for the specified period.

Select the **Period** as **Custom** from the drop-down list, and specify the date range as 01/01/2016 to 31/01/2016 in the **From** and **To** date fields.

The **More** button allows you to refine the report by category, or by a specific ledger account. You can select the ledger account from the drop-down list in the **Ledger Account** field.

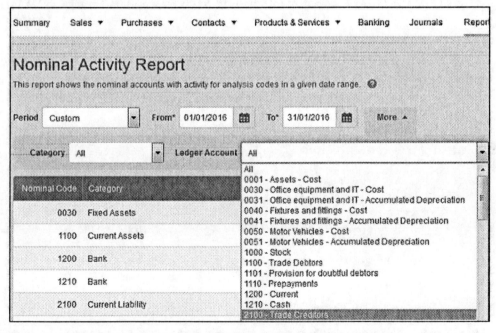

To see each transaction in the selected nominal ledger account, click on the summary line for that account to view the detailed activity.

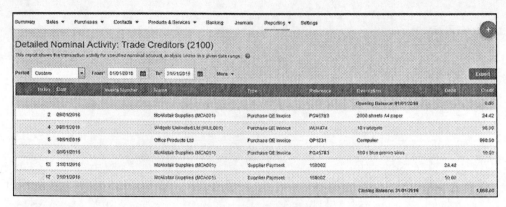

Use the **Export** button to export the report as a PDF file and save it to your computer. Please refer to the 'Exporting to PDF file' section in Chapter 3 for details on how to do this.

Audit Trail

The **Audit Trail** report provides a detailed breakdown of all transactions posted to Sage One. This can be accessed by choosing **Reporting > Audit Trail.** This brings up a summary report. Click on the **Detailed** button to get the detailed report.

> Detailed

The detailed report looks similar to this:

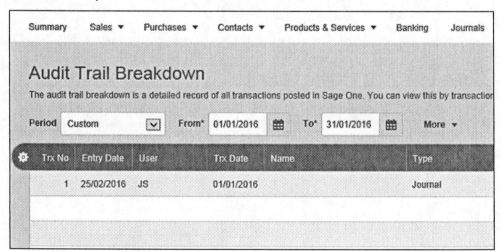

BPP LEARNING MEDIA

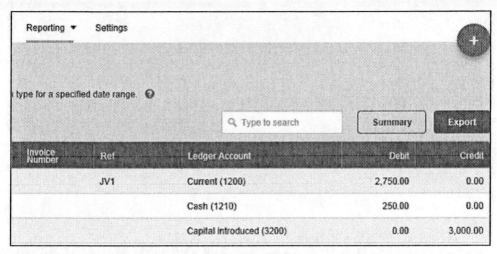

You should ensure that the date range covers every transaction you have entered. To specify the date range, select **Custom** from the **Period** drop-down list and specify the date range in the **From** Date and **To** Date fields.

This will generate a list of all the transactions, numbered in the order in which you posted them. If you need to, you are also able to refine the report by a particular type of transaction, eg journals, by clicking on the **More** button and then selecting **Journal** from the drop-down list in the **Type** field, as shown below.

You can search for a particular transaction by entering the amount of the transaction or, more specifically, the transaction reference in the search box.

Generating an Audit Trail report is also a syllabus requirement, and part of this requirement is for the report to show bank reconciled transactions. This can be done on the Audit Trail report by adding a specific column for bank reconciled transactions. To do this, click the button that looks like a cog at the left end of the menu bar as shown below.

This brings up the following selection of columns. Click on the check-box next to the **Bank Reconciled** option.

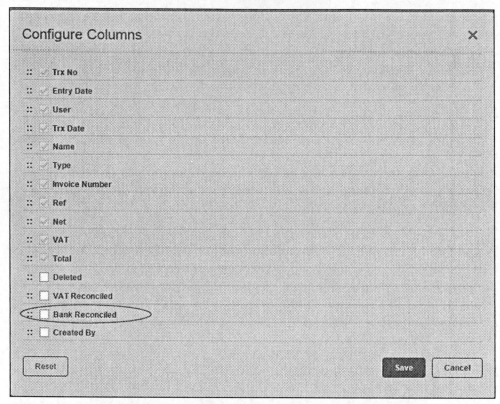

A column entitled **Bank Reconciled** is now included in the report.

Ledger Account	Debit	Credit	Bank Reconci
Current (1200)	2,750.00	0.00	Yes

Note. If you cannot see the **Bank Reconciled** column at this stage, you may need to reduce the size of the screen by holding the **Ctrl** and **–** keys at the same time.

Use the **Export** button to export the report as a PDF file and save it to your computer. Please refer to the 'Exporting to PDF file' section in Chapter 3 for details on how to do this.

3.3 Invoices and statements

Some reports, such as invoices and statements, may be intended to be printed on pre-printed stationery. Remember that when you preview these documents on

screen, you will see words and figures on plain paper. This is obvious if you think about it, but we mention it because it surprises some new users.

To produce a customer statement, choose the customer by **Contacts > Customers >** click on the customer > **Manage > Statements**.

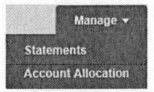

Select the date you want the statement up to in the **To** field and the statement appears on screen.

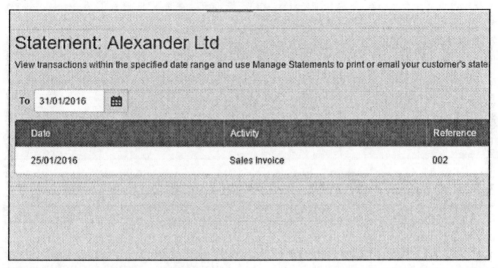

Clicking on **Manage Statement** gives you options for the output of the statement.

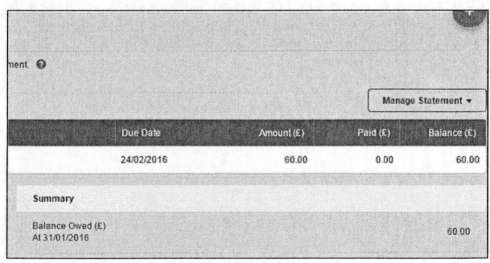

You should select **Print** and this will generate the statement in a new window in your internet browser. You can then save the statement as a PDF file to your computer using the menu in your internet browser.

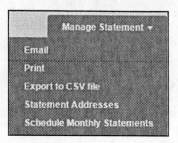

3.4 Reports in assessments

The following table lists the reports you may be asked for in an assessment, with brief instructions explaining how to obtain them in Sage One. Make sure that you select appropriate dates for your reports in the **Period** field and don't forget to save the reports as PDF files to your computer.

REPORT DESCRIPTION	REPORT NAME (Sage One)	WHERE TO FIND IT
Balance owed from each customer	Aged Debtors	**Reporting > Aged Debtors > Detailed > Export > PDF**
Balance owed to each supplier	Aged Creditors	**Reporting > Aged Creditors > Detailed > Export > PDF**
A list of balances all nominal ledger accounts	Trial Balance	**Reporting > Trial Balance > Export > PDF**
A list of customer invoices and credit notes	Sales Day Book (includes Sales Returns)	**Reporting > Sales Day Book > Export > PDF**
A list of supplier invoices and credit notes	Purchase Day Book (includes Purchases returns)	**Reporting > Purchases Day Book > Export > PDF**

REPORT DESCRIPTION	REPORT NAME (Sage One)	WHERE TO FIND IT
All transactions with each customer	Customer Activity	**Contacts > Customers >** click on the check box next to the required customer **> More > Activity Report > Generate** To select all customers, click on the check box on the menu bar next to 'Company/Name'. Note that receipts allocated to transactions in the customer accounts are identifiable as they have 0.00 in the 'Outstanding' column.
All transactions with each supplier	Supplier Activity	**Contacts > Suppliers >** click on the check box next to the required supplier **> More > Activity Report > Generate** To select all suppliers, click on the check box on the menu bar next to 'Company/Name'. Note that payments allocated to items in the supplier accounts are identifiable as they have 0.00 in the 'Outstanding' column.
Statements of account to credit customers	Customer Statements	**Contacts > Customers >** click on the required customer **> Manage > Statements > Manage Statement > Print**
Advice of payment to a supplier showing invoice(s) paid	Remittance Advice	**Banking >** click on the required bank account **> Activity > click on the required payment > Print remittance (drop down next to Save button)**

REPORT DESCRIPTION	REPORT NAME (Sage One)	WHERE TO FIND IT
Audit trail – a list of every transaction entered into Sage including journal entries in order of entry.	Audit trail	**Reporting > Audit Trail > Detailed > Export > PDF** If you can only see the 'Summary' button, this means you are already in the detailed report. Make sure that you configure the columns in this report to include 'Bank Reconciled' transactions as described earlier in the Audit Trail Report section earlier.
All transactions within nominal ledger accounts	Nominal Activity	**Reporting > Nominal Activity > Export > PDF** This will generate a report for all Nominal ledger codes. To generate a report for one account, click on **More** and select the required ledger code from the **Ledger account** field.
Comparison of bank statement balance to bank nominal ledger account balance	Bank reconciliation	**Banking >** click on the required account > **Reconciliations >** click on the required reconciliation > **Print**
List of payments and receipts made from the bank account	Receipts & Payments Day Book	**Reporting > Receipts & Payments Day Book > More>** select required bank account > **Receipt/Payment > Export> PDF**

* Note. The syllabus requires you to generate an Audit Trail report to include details of all transactions, including details of items in the bank account that have been reconciled, and details of receipts/payments allocated to items in customer/supplier accounts. The Audit Trail report on Sage One does not indicate that receipts/payments have been allocated to items in the customer/supplier accounts. To get around this, you can run the **Customer/Supplier Activity** report, as described in the table above. Receipts/payments allocated to items in the customer/supplier accounts are identifiable, as they have 0.00 in the **Outstanding** column.

Task 6

Set up another customer as follows:

Springsteen Ltd
223 Home Town
Bradford
BD11 3EE

Process a sales invoice, Invoice no. 003, to this customer for £600 (net) for 20 Super-widgets, VAT at standard rate, invoice dated 26 January 2016.

Task 7

You notice that on 15 January the bank has debited your current account £10 for bank charges (no VAT). Enter this transaction.

On 31 January the bank credits you with £0.54 interest (no VAT). Rather than net this off against the Bank charges and interest account, you decide to set up a new nominal ledger account: Bank interest received, in the Other income category. Set up the new account and enter the transaction for the interest received.

Task 8

Go to **Reporting > Aged Debtors > Detailed**. Run the report up to 31/01/2016.

Export the report to a PDF and save it to your computer.

Open the PDF version and review your report. It should show all invoices as current.

3.5 Transfers

To transfer between bank accounts, including petty cash (cash in hand), you use the **Bank Transfer** option. For example, to transfer £100 from the bank current account to the cash in hand account, select **Banking > New Entry > Bank Transfer**. Select the **Paid from** bank account as the current account, and the **Paid into** bank account as the cash in hand account. Enter the date that the money was transferred in the **Amount Transferred** field. You may find it helpful to enter TRANS in the **Reference** field.

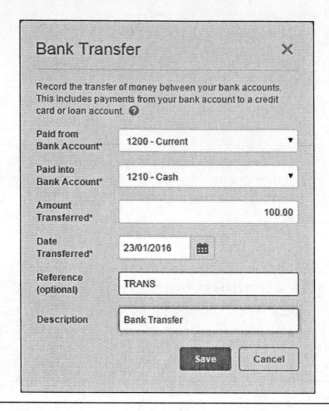

Bank Transfer   ✕

Record the transfer of money between your bank accounts.
This includes payments from your bank account to a credit
card or loan account. ❓

Paid from Bank Account*	1200 - Current ▾
Paid into Bank Account*	1210 - Cash ▾
Amount Transferred*	100.00
Date Transferred*	23/01/2016 📅
Reference (optional)	TRANS
Description	Bank Transfer

Save   Cancel

Task 9

On 23 January, you transfer £100 from the bank account into petty cash and immediately spend:

- £20 on train fares (zero rated for VAT)

- £10 (gross amount) on coffee mugs for the office (standard rated). The net cost of the mugs should be debited to General Expenses

Enter the above transactions.

Task 10

Extract a trial balance for all transactions up to 31/01/2016. If you wish, you can also preview a statement of financial position (balance sheet) and statement of profit or loss (profit and loss account). You will not have to do this in your case study, but they are easy documents to produce and it seems a pity not to have a look!

Reporting > Balance Sheet Report for the balance sheet

Reporting > Profit & Loss for the profit and loss account

Your trial balance in Task 10 should look similar to the one that follows:

Nominal Code	Name	Selected Period Debit	Selected Period Credit
0030	Office equipment and IT - Cost	800.00	
1100	Trade Debtors	780.00	
1200	Current	2,646.12	
1210	Cash	320.00	
2100	Trade Creditors		1,056.00
2200	VAT on Sales		170.00
2201	VAT on Purchases	183.41	
3200	Capital introduced		3,000.00
4000	Sales - products		800.00
5010	Cost of sales - materials	80.00	
7100	Rent and rates	200.00	
7400	Travel and Entertainment	20.00	
7500	Office costs	8.33	
7900	Bank charges and interest	10.00	
8200	General Expenses	8.33	
10000	Publicity material	20.35	
10001	Sales - services		50.00
10003	Bank interest received		0.54
	TOTAL	£5,076.54	£5,076.54

4 Error correction

If you make an error when you are making your entries, it is relatively easy to correct.

Errors made when setting up customer and supplier accounts can be corrected simply by opening the relevant record and changing the data.

For transaction errors, some accounting software programs have the option of correcting transactions by amending the original entry. In Sage One, this option is available but cannot be done in certain circumstances, eg if an invoice has been allocated to a payment. Therefore, as a standard approach, we recommend correcting transactions with another transaction (eg a credit note, journal entry), rather than amending the original transaction. Besides, this is best practice in order to keep a clear audit trail.

Customer invoices

If you have made a mistake on a customer invoice which has been posted, you need to create a credit note, either for the full amount and reissue the invoice, or for the difference. Credit notes are covered in Chapter 3.

Supplier invoices

If a mistake is made by a supplier on an invoice, they will normally send you a credit note, again either for the full amount, with a reissued invoice, or for the difference.

If you have made the mistake yourself, then you need to cancel the invoice, by entering a credit note with the same details.

Credit notes are covered in Chapter 3.

Other entries

Other entries should be corrected by journal entry. Students should also be able to post journal entries to correct their own errors that may occur during the assessment. The journal entry is covered in Chapter 3. For a clear audit trail, it is best practice to post a journal entry to reverse the original entry and then post a journal to re-do the transaction correctly.

Task 11

Let's say that the £20 payment entered in petty cash for a train fare should actually have been £15.

Correct this using a journal entry.

---

5 Irrecoverable debts

In the assessment you might be required to post a journal to write off an irrecoverable debt.

An irrecoverable debt or 'bad debt' as it is sometimes called, is a balance owing from a customer for invoices that will not be paid, perhaps because the customer has gone bankrupt or due to a dispute. Therefore the original invoice amount(s) needs to be written-off in the accounts.

The journal entry to write off an irrecoverable debt is as follows.

		£	£
DEBIT	Irrecoverable (bad) debt expense	GROSS AMT	
CREDIT	Customer account in trade receivables (debtors) ledger		GROSS AMT

Write-off an irrecoverable debt using a credit note

However, in Sage One you cannot use the journal function to post the entry above, as you cannot post directly to the customer account.

(Remember that each customer account is a subsidiary account of the overall trade debtors account, eg, customer account ALE001 is a subsidiary account of the overall trade debtors account – A/C 1100: 'Trade debtors' in Sage One).

Instead, you must use the credit note function. This was referred to in Chapter 3. To recap, select **Sales > Quick Entries > New Quick Entry.**

You are presented with the **Quick entries** screen. The entries you make will be similar to those for entering a sales credit note (ie, selecting **Cr Note** in the **Type** field), but with the following differences.

Ledger Account – select A/C 8100: 'Bad debts' (If this account is not available, ensure you tick the option: **Sales – Invoice / Credit, Product / Services / Customer defaults** in the **Visibility** section of the Edit Ledger Account function, described in the section under Task 3 in Chapter 3).

Net – enter the GROSS amount of the invoice(s) you are writing off

VAT Rate – select 'No VAT' as VAT does not apply at this stage.

For example, let's say you received notification that the customer Alexander Ltd has gone bankrupt, and therefore the balance of £60.00 (gross amt) for invoice no. 002 (created in Task 10, Chapter 3) will not be paid. You would enter the following transaction.

VAT treatment

The VAT treatment above might seem odd at first. You might expect that if you already paid VAT on the original invoice, you can now reclaim that VAT, by entering the net amount, and selecting the VAT Rate as Standard.

However VAT is not reclaimable on all bad debts, as there is a time limit. To comply with current HMRC guidelines, the gross amount is initially posted to the bad debts account, and if VAT is reclaimable, the VAT is separately transferred from the bad debts account to the VAT on purchases account.

6 Month-end procedures

In business there additional procedures that need to be performed at month-end. The main procedures are:

- Post prepayments
- Post accruals
- Post depreciation
- Close the month to prevent posting of further transactions

You do not have to perform these tasks in the Assessment but it is useful to be aware of these as you will undoubtedly encounter them in the workplace and/or future studies.

6.1 Starting over

All of us can have a bad day sometimes! Occasionally, you may find that you or someone else using the software has made a number of mistakes, perhaps due to a misunderstanding.

If this happens, it may well be better to start again rather than trying to correct all the mistakes, possibly making things worse. This can be done by resetting the data, as described in the Assessments section in Chapter 3. This is not normal practice in business of course; however, this function is purely for the Education market.

Note. This option should be taken as a last resort since it will erase all data, including any customers, suppliers and nominal codes you have set up.

Chapter overview

- Payments and receipts should be allocated to outstanding invoices, as it is important to know which invoices have been paid.

- Bank reconciliations are very important controls in accounting systems and are easily accomplished in Sage One.

- All the reports that you are likely to require are available as pre-prepared reports.

- There are facilities for error correction, but it is best not to make errors in the first place!

Keywords

- **Bank reconciliation:** a checking process, whereby differences between an organisation's cash book entries, and the bank issued statement are identified. This gives assurance that the cash book is accurate

- **Customer:** a person or organisation that buys products or services from your organisation

- **Customer record:** the details relating to the customer account, for example name and address, contact details and credit terms

- **Payment allocations:** matching payments (either received or made) to relevant invoices and credit notes

- **Remittance advice:** document that lists all transactions that are being settled by a payment

- **Recurring payments:** payments (or receipts) that are made on a regular, periodic basis. Common examples are standing orders and directy debits

- **Reports:** form that summarises or analyses data that has been input to a computer system

- **Supplier:** a person or organisation that your organisation buys products or services from

- **Supplier record:** the details relating to the supplier account, for example name and address, contact details and credit terms

- **Trade creditors ledger:** the collection of supplier accounts, also known as the purchase ledger

- **Trade debtors ledger:** the collection of customer accounts, also known as the sales ledger

- **Unallocated payments:** payments or parts of payments that cannot be matched to specific transactions

1   When you receive a payment from an account customer, this is posted using the Other Receipts button. True or false? Explain your answer.

2   Which report would you run to view the transactions posted to a particular ledger account?

3   Why can you not see supplier accounts on the nominal activity report?

4   Which report would you run to view the invoices and payments posted to a particular supplier account?

5   Transfers between bank accounts should always be processed by using the Journal facility. True or false?

6   Assuming VAT is applicable in both cases; why do you need to account for VAT on the receipt of payment for a cash sale, but not the receipt of payment for a credit sale?

Answers to chapter tasks

Chapter 1 Sage 50 – Part 1

Task 1

This is a hands-on activity. You need to start either with a new instance of Sage, or a blank company.

Task 2

This is a hands-on activity. The Name should be Publicity material, the Type is Overheads, the Category is Printing and Stationery. Sage will suggest a Ref (account number) such as 7504 or 7506, and you should accept this. There is no opening balance to enter.

Task 3

Vimal could easily forget to give the account a proper name next time he uses the package and in future, he may not have any idea what sort of expense should be recorded in that account. Nobody else who uses the system will have a clue either. The moral of the story is, don't use abbreviations that others might not understand, and take care with spelling too. A bit of care will save time in the long run.

Task 4

It is possible for a customer and a supplier to have the same code, because it is quite possible that a business will both sell and buy goods from the same person. Although the accounts would use the same code, the accounts would be held in different ledgers.

Task 5

This is a hands-on activity. Use the **New** button or the **Wizard** button in the **Suppliers** function and fill in as much detail as possible. When you have finished, open your record and check the details on screen against those given. The illustration in the Task shows the code MCA001 (consistent with the alphanumeric format recommended earlier in the chapter).

Task 6

This is a hands-on activity. You can check that you have performed this action correctly by reviewing the supplier record; the defaults tab should show the nominal code for Publicity Material.

Task 7

This is a hands-on activity. Make sure that your journal has an appropriate reference and that each line has a description (use the F6 key for the second two lines).

You can check your journal by clicking the **Transactions** button or by looking at the activity of the nominal ledger accounts affected (**Nominal Codes >** select the nominal code **> Activity**.

Task 8

This is a hands-on activity. If you exit the program as suggested, remember to reset the date to 31/1/16 when you relaunch Sage.

Task 9

This is a hands-on activity. (Use the F6 key when entering the second line of the invoice, to save typing.) The total VAT is £5.74 (£4.07 on the first item, which was given **net**, and £1.67 on the second, where we told you the **gross** amount). Don't forget that you can use the F9 button to calculate the net amount.

Task 10

This is a hands-on activity. You should have set up the two suppliers, remembering to tick the 'terms agreed' box in the credit control tab (or in the wizard). You could also have changed the default nominal code for Office Products Ltd to Office Equipment (0030), as this is the type of purchase we have made from them. After setting up the two suppliers, you should have clicked on 'batch invoice' and entered these two transactions as per Task 9. After the task is complete, you should see a balance of £1,090.42 on your creditors control account.

Task 11

This is a hands-on activity. You should have decided to post the different types of sales (one was products, one was a service) to different sales accounts. You should have renamed the standard sales accounts in Sage to suit your particular business.

Chapter 2 Sage 50 – Part 2

Task 1

This is a credit transaction so use the 'supplier payment' option, <u>not</u> the 'bank payment' option.

Choose: Bank Accounts > Supplier Payments.

Task 2

This is a credit transaction so use the 'customer receipt' option, <u>not</u> the 'bank receipt' option.

Choose: Bank Accounts > Customer Receipts.

Task 3

Choose: Bank accounts > Recurring Items > Add.

The details you enter should match those shown in the Add/Edit Recurring Entry screen shot above Task 3 in Chapter 2 of the Text.

Task 4

Choose: Bank Accounts > Recurring Items, select the recurring payment and click on Process. Before you click on Process, the Postings Made column should show 0. Once you have processed the payment, the Postings Made column should show 1.

Task 5

To access the bank reconciliation screen choose: Bank Accounts > Select current account > Reconcile.

Follow the steps outlined in the Bank Reconciliation section of the Text, and check that your reconciliation matches that shown in the screen shot.

The only reconciling item between the bank statement balance (£2,790.00) and the ledger balance (£2,755.58) should be the payment to McAlistair Supplies of £34.42. The other bank transactions should be as reconciled.

Task 6

A new customer can be set up by choosing: Customers > New/Edit.

Task 7

Make sure you set up the new ledger account first. This can be done in the same way as in Task 2 in Chapter 1 (ie, click on Nominal Codes from the left side of the screen, and then click on the Wizard button).

Task 8

Run the aged debtors report as instructed in the task, ie, Customers > Reports > Aged Debtors. You can export to a PDF file by clicking on the Export button, and saving to your computer.

Task 9

Firstly, use the bank transfer function to transfer £100 from the current account to the petty cash account. Choose: Bank Accounts > Bank Transfer.

The 'from' account' is 1200: Bank Current Account, and the 'to' account is 1230: Petty Cash.

Secondly, use the 'bank payment' function in the same way as in Task 1 above. Remember to select the correct tax code.

Note that you are given the gross amount for the coffee mugs. In Sage 50, you can enter the gross amount, and then press F9; the program will automatically calculate the VAT (of £1.67).

Task 10

Choose: Nominal Codes, > Reports > Trial Balance.

Select the period as Month 1, January 2016.

Check that your Trial Balance matches that shown in the Text. If there are differences, go back and work out where you were wrong. You can correct your errors using the methods described in the Error Correction section in Chapter 2 of the Text.

Task 11

Choose: Nominal Codes > Journal Entry. It is best practice to post a journal to reverse the incorrect entry, and then post another journal for the correct entry.

The reversal of the original entry is:

DEBIT	1230 – Petty Cash	20.00	
CREDIT	7400 – Travelling		20.00

The correct entry is:

DEBIT	7400 – Travelling	15.00	
CREDIT	1230 – Petty Cash		15.00

Chapter 3 Sage One – Part 1

Task 1

This is a hands-on activity. You need to start either with a new instance of Sage, or a blank company.

Task 2

This is a hands-on activity. The Ledger Name and Display Name should be Publicity material, the Category is Overheads. Sage will suggest a Nominal Code (account number) such as 10000 or 10001, and you should accept this. The opening balance is not entered at this stage.

Task 3

Vimal could easily forget to give the account a proper name next time he uses the package and in future, he may not have any idea what sort of expense should be recorded in that account. Nobody else who uses the system will have a clue either. The moral of the story is, don't use abbreviations that others might not understand, and take care with spelling too. A bit of care will save time in the long run.

Task 4

It is possible for a customer and a supplier to have the same code, because it is quite possible that a business will both sell and buy goods from the same person. Although the accounts would use the same code, the accounts would be held in different ledgers.

Task 5

This is a hands-on activity. Use New Supplier button and fill in as much detail as possible. When you have finished, open your record and check the details on screen against those given. The illustration in the Task shows the code MCA001 (consistent with the alphanumeric format recommended earlier in the chapter).

Task 6

This is a hands-on activity. The following fields should read as follows if you have performed this correctly: 'Set Credit Limit (£)': 5,000.00; 'Purchase Ledger Account': 10000 – Publicity material; and the 'Use default terms' field should be selected.

Task 7

This is a hands-on activity. Make sure that your journal has an appropriate reference and that each line has a description.

You can check your journal by generating the Audit trail report, or by generating the Nominal Activity report and looking at the detail of the nominal ledger accounts affected, if you wish.

Task 8

This is a hands-on activity. The total VAT is £5.74 (£4.07 on the first item, which was given **net**, and £1.67 on the second, where we told you the **gross** amount). You can calculate the net amount by dividing the gross amount by (1 + VAT rate), ie £10.00 / 1.20.

Task 9

This is a hands-on activity. You should have set up the two suppliers, remembering to tick the 'terms agreed' box in the credit control tab (or in the wizard). You could also have changed the default nominal code for Office Products Ltd to 'Office Equipment and IT – Cost' (0030), as this is the type of purchase we have made from them. After setting up the two suppliers, you should have clicked on 'batch invoice' and entered these two transactions as per Task 9. After the task is complete, you should see a balance of £1,090.42 on your creditors control account.

Task 10

This is a hands-on activity. You should have decided to post the different types of sales (one was products, one was a service) to different sales accounts. You should have renamed the standard sales accounts in Sage to suit your particular business.

Task 11

This is a hands-on activity. Check your final balance to the one shown at the activity.

Chapter 4 Sage One – Part 2

Task 1

This is a credit transaction so use the 'supplier payment' option, <u>not</u> the 'other payment' option.

Choose: Banking > Select current account > New Entry > Purchase/Payment > Supplier Payment.

Task 2

This is a credit transaction so use the 'customer receipt' option, <u>not</u> the 'other receipt' option.

Choose: Banking > Select current account > New Entry > Sale/Receipt > Customer Receipt.

Task 3

You can create the first payment using the 'other payment function'.

Task 4

You can find the payment you made in Task 3 in the Activity screen within Banking.

Choose: Banking > Select current account > Activity.

Make sure that the dates in the From and To boxes are around the time of payment (15 January 2016), otherwise it will not show.

Clicking on the payment will show the details of the payment, including a 'Make Recurring' button. Click on this button to enter and save the details of the recurrence.

Task 5

To access the bank reconciliation screen choose: Banking > Select current account > Click on the drop-down arrow next to Connect to Bank > Reconcile.

Follow the steps outlined in the Bank Reconciliation section in the Text, and check that your reconciliation matches that shown in the screen shot.

The only reconciling item between the bank statement balance (£2,790.00) and the ledger balance (£2,755.58) should be the payment to McAlistair Supplies of £34.42. The other bank transactions should be as reconciled.

Task 6

A new customer can be set up by choosing: Contacts > Customer > New Customer.

Task 7

Make sure you set up the new ledger account first. This can be done in the same way as in Task 2 in Chapter 3 (ie, choose: Settings > Chart of Accounts > New Ledger Account).

Task 8

Run the aged debtors report as instructed in the task, ie, Reporting > Aged Debtors > Detailed. You can export to a PDF file by choosing: Export > PDF, which will generate a PDF version which you can save to your computer.

Task 9

Firstly, use the bank transfer function to transfer £100 from the current account to the petty cash account. Choose: Banking > Select Current account > New Entry > Bank Transfer. The 'paid from account' is 1200: Current, and the 'paid to account' is 1210: Cash.

Secondly, use the 'other payment' function in the same way as in Task 1 above. Remember to select the correct VAT rates.

Note that you are given the <u>gross</u> amount for the coffee mugs. In Sage One, you should enter the gross amount, as the program will automatically calculate the VAT (of £1.67) and post it to the VAT on purchases account.

Task 10

Choose: Reporting > Trial Balance.

Select the Period as Custom and enter From: 01/01/2016 To: 31/01/2016.

Check that your Trial Balance matches that shown in the Text. If there are differences, go back and work out where you wrong. You can correct your errors using the methods described in the Error Correction section in Chapter 4 of the Text.

Task 11

Choose: Journals > New Journal. It is best practice to post a journal to reverse the incorrect entry, and then post another journal for the correct entry.

The reversal of the original entry is:

DEBIT	1210 – Cash	20.00	
CREDIT	7400 – Travel and entertainment		20.00

The correct entry is:

DEBIT	7400 – Travel and entertainment	15.00	
CREDIT	1210 – Cash		15.00

Test your learning: answers

Chapter 1 Sage 50 – Part 1

1 A field is a box on screen in which you enter data or select from a list (similar to a spreadsheet cell).

2 A default is the entry that the accounting package knows will normally be made in a particular field – for example, today's date or the nominal code that a purchase from a certain supplier would normally be posted to.

3 The chart of accounts is a kind of template setting out the structure of the nominal ledger – which accounts are classed as non-current (fixed) assets, which are current assets, which are current liabilities, which are expenses in the statement of profit or loss (income statement), and so on.

4 You must set up an account for the supplier in the purchase ledger before you can post an invoice received from the supplier.

5 You can either set a default nominal ledger expenditure account when you set up the supplier account, or you can choose the nominal ledger account at the time that you post the invoice.

6 This is false. The system will not allow you to post a journal that does not balance.

7 It is usually better to post the invoice lines individually. It is essential to do so if the individual expenses need to be posted to different nominal ledger codes.

Chapter 2 Sage 50 - Part 2

1   This is false. Receipts from customers with accounts need to be allocated to outstanding invoices. From the **Bank accounts** menu, these receipts are processed using the **Customer Receipt** button.

2   The **Nominal Activity report** shows the transactions that have been posted to each nominal ledger account.

3   Supplier accounts are subsidiary accounts of the **Trade Creditors account**. Therefore, supplier **transactions** are posted to this one account.

4   The **Supplier Activity report** shows the transactions that have been posted to each supplier account.

5   False. The transfer should be processed by selecting **Bank accounts**, selecting the required bank account and then selecting **Bank Transfer**.

6   For a credit sale, VAT is accounted for on the sales invoice sent to the customer, and not the subsequent receipt of payment by the customer. For a cash sale, the sale and receipt of payment occur at the same time in one transaction; therefore, VAT must be accounted for at this point.

Chapter 3 Sage One – Part 1

1   A field is a box on screen in which you enter data or select from a list (similar to a spreadsheet cell).

2   A default is the entry that the accounting package knows will normally be made in a particular field, for example, today's date or the nominal code that a purchase from a certain supplier would normally be posted to.

3   The chart of accounts is a kind of template setting out the structure of the nominal ledger – which accounts are classed as non-current (fixed) assets, which are current assets, which are current liabilities, which are expenses in the statement of profit or loss (income statement), and so on.

4   You must set up an account for the supplier in the purchase ledger before you can post an invoice received from the supplier.

5   You can either set a default nominal ledger account when you set up the supplier account, or you can choose the nominal ledger account at the time that you post the invoice.

6   This is false. The system will not allow you to post a journal that does not balance.

7   It is usually better to post the invoice lines individually. It is essential to do so if the individual expenses need to be posted to different nominal ledger codes.

Chapter 4 Sage One – Part 2

1   This is false. Receipts from customers with accounts need to be allocated to outstanding invoices using the **Customer Receipt** function. This is accessed from **Banking > Clicking on the required bank account > New Entry > Sale/Receipt > Customer Receipt**.

2   The **Nominal Activity report** shows the transactions that have been posted to each nominal ledger account.

3   Supplier accounts are subsidiary accounts of the **Trade Creditors account**. Therefore, supplier **transactions** are posted to this one account.

4   The **Supplier Activity report** shows the transactions that have been posted to each supplier account.

5   False. The transfer should be processed by selecting **Banking**, clicking on the required bank account and then selecting **Bank Transfer** from the **New Entry** drop-down list. Note that the transfer option is also available from the **New Entry** drop down list in the main **banking** screen

6   For a credit sale, VAT is accounted for on the sales invoice sent to the customer, and not the subsequent receipt of payment by the customer. For a cash sale, the sale and receipt of payment occur at the same time in one transaction; therefore, VAT must be accounted for at this point.

AAT AQ2016 SAMPLE ASSESSMENT USING ACCOUNTING SOFTWARE

Time allowed: 2 hours

Using Accounting Software
AAT sample assessment

Assessment information:

The time allowed to complete this assessment is **2 hours.**

This assessment consists of **13 tasks** and it is important that you attempt them all.

- You will be asked to produce documents and reports to demonstrate your competence.

- You must then upload these documents so they can be marked by AAT.

All documents must be uploaded within the **total time** available. It is important that you upload **all** reports and documents specified in the tasks so your work can be assessed.

You will be able to attach and remove files throughout the duration of this assessment until you click on 'Finish', which will submit your assessment.

All uploaded documents should be saved and titled with the following information:

- evidence number
- your name
- your AAT membership number.

The evidence number to use for each document is stated in the table in Task 13.

Example

Your name is Simon White, and your AAT membership number is: 12345678

Evidence 1

A document showing all of the purchase invoices and credit notes (by purchase type) posted in June 20XX.

This document would be saved and uploaded as: Evidence 1 – Simon White – 12345678

If multiple documents are uploaded to show competency in an individual task, name these Evidence 1A and Evidence 1B and so on.

Unless the assessment asks for a specific format, you can choose the format which will best enable the marker to review and assess your work.

During the assessment, you will only make entries to the nominal ledger accounts you created in Task 3. You will not be required to make any entries to any accounts other than those you have already created.

Information

The Graze Office Store is a UK furniture business. The business sells a mix of new and second-hand office furniture and has been trading successfully for five years. The owner, Kate Allen, has always used spreadsheets to carry out routine bookkeeping tasks. However the business has grown significantly over the last 12 months and Kate has decided to start using an accounting software package from 1 June 20XX onwards

Information relating to the business:

Business name:	The Graze Office Store
Business address:	1 Hope Street Cathertown Lumley LM61 2RT
Business owner:	Kate Allen
Accounting period end:	31 May (each year)
VAT Number:	781163367 (standard scheme)
VAT rate:	Standard rate VAT of 20% charged on all sales

Sales

Most of The Graze Office Store's income is generated from online sales where customers pay through an online payment system. The business also sells its items to other business in the north and south of the United Kingdom.

Kate likes to keep a record of the different sales made by the business, by sales type:

- online sales
- sales to shops - North
- sales to shops - South

You have been asked to carry out the bookkeeping tasks for June 20XX **only**, the first month that the business will be using computerised accounting software and the start of the new accounting period.

All documents have been checked for accuracy and have been authorised by Kate Allen.

Before you start the assessment you should:

- Set the system software date as 30 June of the current year.
- Set the financial year to start on 1 June of the current year.

Task 1 (3 marks)

Refer to the customer listing below and set up customer records to open sales ledger accounts for each customer, entering opening balances at 1 June 20XX.

Customer listing

Customer name and address	Customer account code	Customer account details at 1 June 20XX
Giffall Recruitment 3 High Street Meadowville ME2 6US	GIF001	Opening balance: £844.26 Payment term: 30 days
Happy Engineers Ltd 27 The Grange Totton TT21 2SA	HAP001	Opening balance: £1,425.65 Payment term: 30 days
Perry Cars 25 Edge Avenue Jeanpurt JE3 8TY	PER001	Opening balance: £4,680.00 Payment term: 45 days

Task 2 (3 marks)

Refer to the supplier listing below and set up supplier records to open purchase ledger accounts for each supplier, entering opening balances at 1 June 20XX.

Supplier listing

Supplier name and address	Supplier account code	Supplier account details at 1 June 20XX
Fabrics Delight Unit 3, The Dome Centre Whittingham Greater Whitt GW2 3TX	FAB001	Opening balance: £1,320.11 Payment term: 60 days

Supplier name and address	Supplier account code	Supplier account details at 1 June 20XX
QC Exclusive Ocean House London NW2 9GY	QCE001	Opening balance: £920.46 Payment term: 30 days
Totally Wood 35 Montpellier Street Great Lowe Georgemarnier GM3 8LD	TOT001	Opening balance: £135.56 Payment term: 30 days

Task 3 (19 marks)

Refer to the list of nominal ledger accounts below taken from the spreadsheet that the business has been using.

Set up nominal ledger records for each account, entering opening balances (if applicable) at 1 June 20XX, ensuring you select, amend or create appropriate nominal ledger account codes.

Opening Trial Balance as at 1 June 20XX

Account names	Note	Debit balance £	Credit balance £
Computer equipment – cost		4,600.00	
Computer equipment – accumulated depreciation			1,200.00
Delivery vehicles – cost		22,800.00	
Delivery vehicles – accumulated depreciation			5,000.00
Fixtures and fittings – cost		6,445.00	
Fixtures and fittings – accumulated depreciation			1,625.00
Bank current account		13,984.24	
Petty cash		75.00	
Sales ledger control account	1	6,949.91	

Account names	Note	Debit balance £	Credit balance £
Purchase ledger control account	1		2,376.13
Sales tax control account	2		12,100.00
Purchase tax control account	2	7,540.00	
Capital			40,093.02
Online sales	3		NIL
Sales to shops – North	3		NIL
Sales to shops – South	3		NIL
Purchases – completed units	3	NIL	
Purchases – raw materials	3	NIL	
Wages	3	NIL	
Rent and rates	3	NIL	
Electricity	3	NIL	
Delivery vehicle expenses	3	NIL	
Bank charges	3	NIL	
Stationery	3	NIL	
Travel and subsistence	3	NIL	
		62,394.15	62,394.15

Notes

1 As the individual customer and supplier balances have already been posted, the accounting software you are using may require you to make a separate adjustment for these.

2 The software you are using may not require you to post these balances individually. The opening balance on the account is £4,560 (credit) if posting as a single brought forward balance.

3 These nominal accounts are needed for transactions taking place in June 20XX.

In the rest of the assessment, you will only make entries to the nominal ledger accounts you created in Task 3. You will not be required to make any entries to any accounts other than those you have already created.

BPP
LEARNING MEDIA

Task 4 (15 marks)

Refer to the following summary of sales invoices and summary of sales credit notes. Enter these transactions into the accounting software, ensuring you enter all the information below and select the correct sales code.

Summary of sales invoices

Date	Customer	Invoice number	Gross £	VAT £	Net £	Sales analysis £	
						Shop sales – North	Shop sales – South
6 June	Happy Engineers Ltd	HAP001/IN24	960.00	160.00	800.00	800.00	
12 June	Giffall Recruitment	GIF001/IN17	510.00	85.00	425.00	425.00	
24 June	Perry Cars	PER001/IN4	2,460.00	410.00	2,050.00		2,050.00
28 June	Happy Engineers Ltd	HAP001/IN25	2,237.94	372.99	1,864.95	1,864.95	
Totals			6,167.94	1,027.99	5,139.95	3,089.95	2,050.00

Summary of sales credit notes

Date	Customer	Invoice number	Gross £	VAT £	Net £	Sales analysis £	
						Shop sales – North	Shop sales – South
26 June	Happy Engineers Ltd	HAP001/C6*	186.00	31.00	155.00	155.00	
Totals			186.00	31.00	155.00	155.00	

* The credit note relates to some items on invoice HAP001/IN24.

● ●

Task 5 (9 marks)

Refer to the following purchase invoices and the purchase credit note and enter these transactions into the accounting software, ensuring you enter all the information below and select the correct purchases code.

Purchase invoices

QC Exclusive　　　　　**Date: 1 June 20XX**
Ocean House
London
NW2 9GY
VAT Registration No 554 222 657 14

Invoice No: 365

To:
The Graze Office Store
1 Hope Street
Cathertown
Lumley
LM61 2RT

	£
150 plastic chairs (Net)	**1,500.00**
VAT @ 20%	**300.00**
Total	**1,800.00**

Totally Wood   Date: 12 June 20XX
35 Montpellier Street
Great Lowe
Georgemarnier
GM3 8LD

Invoice No: PRE/14

To:
The Graze Office Store
1 Hope Street
Cathertown
Lumley
LM61 2RT

	£
40 metres of 2 inch plywood (Net)	340.00
VAT @ 20%	68.00
Total	408.00

Purchase credit note

Totally Wood	**Date: 18 June 20XX**
35 Montpellier Street	
Great Lowe	
Georgemarnier	
GM3 8LD	

Credit Note No:
PRE/CN3
Linked to Invoice No: PRE/14

To:
The Graze Office Store
1 Hope Street
Cathertown
Lumley
LM61 2RT

	£
12 metres of 2 inch plywood (Net)	**102.00**
VAT @ 20%	**20.40**
Total	**122.40**
Detail: Inferior quality plywood	

The Graze Office Store sells to most of its customers online. All payments made by customers are done through a secure online payment system called CashChum.

CashChum make payments to The Graze Office Store at the end of each week using 'Faster Payments'.

Task 6a (6 marks)

Refer to the following 'Online cash sales listing' and enter these receipts into the accounting software.

Online cash sales listing for June (Bank receipts)

Week ending	Amount received from CashChum* £
9 June 20XX	4,255.66
16 June 20XX	3,854.25
23 June 20XX	3,614.22
30 June 20XX	1,996.99

*All online sales include VAT at the standard rate.

Task 6b (3 marks)

Refer to the following email from Kate Allen and enter this transaction into the accounting software.

Email	
From:	Kate Allen
To:	Accounting Technician
Date:	16 June 20XX
Subject:	Delivery Drivers Wages

Hi,

Wages for the month are £6,200 and this will be paid today by BACS.

Thanks,

Kate

Task 7 (6 marks)

Refer to the following BACS remittance advices received from customers and enter these transactions into the accounting software, ensuring you allocate all amounts as stated on each remittance advice note.

BACS remittance advices

Happy Engineers

BACS Remittance Advice

To: The Graze Office Store

Date: 22 June 20XX

Amount: £1,425.65

Detail: Payment of balance owed as at 1 June 20XX.

Giffall Recruitment

BACS Remittance Advice

To: The Graze Office Store

Date: 30 June 20XX

Amount: £1,265.00

Detail: Payment of balance owed as at 1 June 20XX plus part payment of invoice number GIF001/IN17.

Task 8 (9 marks)

Refer to the following summary of cheque payments made to credit and cash suppliers. Enter these transactions into the accounting software, ensuring you allocate (where applicable) all amounts as shown in the details column.

Cheques paid listing

Date	Cheque number	Supplier	£	Details
16 June	000294	Fabrics Delight	1,320.11	Payment of opening balance
29 June	000295	Totally Wood	421.16	Payment of opening balance plus Invoice No: PRE/14 and Credit Note No: PRE/CN3
30 June	000296	Mick's Motors*	450.00 (including £75 VAT)	Repair of delivery van and new tyres

*Mick's Motors is not a credit supplier and does not have an account with the business.

Task 9 (4 marks)

Refer to the following standing order schedule below and:

(a) set up the recurring entry for rent

(b) save a screenshot of the screen setting up the recurring entry prior to processing. You will be provided with the required evidence number for this in Task 13.

(c) process the first payment.

Standing order schedule

Details	Amount £	Frequency of payment	Payment start date
Monthly rent	600	Each month	01 June 20XX

Detail:

The owner of the unit block increases the monthly rent charge annually on 1 June.

The recurring payment is set up each year on 1 June and is set up for 12 months. VAT is not applicable.

Task 10 (3 marks)

Refer to the following petty cash vouchers and enter these into the accounting software.

Petty cash vouchers

Date: 9 June 20XX
Name: Jim Murfin
Authorised by: **Kate Allen**
Voucher: 124

	£
Stationery	6.00
VAT	1.20
Total amount	7.20

Date: 9 June 20XX
Name: Sandra Owen
Authorised by: **Kate Allen**
Voucher: 125

	£
Travel for course	14.00 (No VAT)

Date: 14 June 20XX
Name: Suki Joshi
Authorised by: **Kate Allen**
Voucher: 126

	£
Train fare	4.75 (No VAT)

Task 11 (4 marks)

Refer to the following journal entries and enter them into the accounting software.

Journals

Date	Account	Debit £	Credit £
30 June 20XX	Computer equipment – cost	95.00	
30 June 20XX	Fixtures and fittings – cost		95.00

Narrative: Being the correction of an incorrectly coded non-current asset purchase invoice from May.

30 June 20XX	Wages	25.95	
30 June 20XX	Bank current account		25.95

Narrative: Being an error in the wages figure shown in the email on 16 June 20XX.

Task 12 (11 marks)

Refer to the following bank statement. Using the accounting software and the transactions you have already posted:

(a) Enter any additional items on the bank statement that have yet to be recorded, into the accounting software (ignore VAT on any of these transactions).

(b) Reconcile the bank statement. If the bank statement does not reconcile, check your work and make the necessary corrections.

(c) Save a screenshot of the bank reconciliation screen. You will be provided with the required evidence number for this in Task 13.

Bank of Markham
201 Manor Road
Lumley
LM61 2RT

The Graze Office Store
1 Hope Street
Cathertown
Lumley
LM61 2RT

Sort code: 44 - 21 - 09

Account Number: 01872249

Statement date: 30 June 20XX

Statement of account

Date 20XX	Details	Money In £	Money Out £	Balance £
01 June	Opening balance			13,984.24
01 June	SO – Rent		600.00	13,384.24
09 June	FP – CashChum	4,255.66		17,639.90
16 June	Cheque 294		1,320.11	16,319.79
16 June	FP – CashChum	3,854.25		20,174.04
16 June	BACS – Wages		6,225.95	13,948.09
22 June	BACS – Happy Engineers	1,425.65		15,373.74
23 June	FP – CashChum	3,614.22		18,987.96
27 June	DD – Electricity		101.00	18,886.96
28 June	Bank charges		14.00	18,872.96
29 June	Cheque 295		421.16	18,451.80
30 June	BACS – Giffall Recruitment	1,265.00		19,716.80
30 June	FP – CashChum	1,996.99		21,713.79
30 June	Cheque 296		450.00	21,263.79

Task 13 (5 marks)

Documentation of evidence

You are now required to generate the following documents to demonstrate your competence:

Document and reports	Save / upload as:
A document showing all transactions with each customer during June 20XX.	**Evidence 1a** – Name – AAT Number
A document showing the balance owed by each customer as at 30 June 20XX.	**Evidence 1b** – Name – AAT Number
The following information must be evidenced within these documents: • Customer name • Account code • Payment terms	Depending on your software, you may need to upload one or more documents.
A document showing all transactions with each supplier during June 20XX.	**Evidence 2a** – Name – AAT Number
A document showing the balance owed to each supplier as at 30 June 20XX.	**Evidence 2b** – Name – AAT Number
The following information must be evidenced within these documents: • Supplier name • Account code • Payment terms	Depending on your software, you may need to upload one or more documents.
Audit trail, showing full details of all transactions, including details of receipts/payments allocated to items in customer/supplier accounts and details in the bank account that have been reconciled.	**Evidence 3** – Name – AAT Number
Trial balance as at 30 June 20XX.	**Evidence 4** – Name – AAT Number
A screenshot of the recurring entry screen including all relevant input details.	**Evidence 5** – Name – AAT Number
A screenshot of the bank reconciliation screen showing reconciled items.	**Evidence 6** – Name – AAT Number

AAT AQ2016 SAMPLE ASSESSMENT USING ACCOUNTING SOFTWARE

ANSWERS

Using Accounting Software
AAT sample assessment

Answers

The model answers here are not exhaustive. The actual format of the document will be dependent on the accounting software used. Candidates may upload more than once piece of documentary evidence per task.

Evidence 1a/1b

The answer provided below shows all of the information required. The candidate may upload more than one piece of evidence.

Customer: Giffall Recruitment

Account: GIF001

Terms: 30 days

Date	Detail	Debit £	Credit £	Balance £
1 June 20XX	Opening balance	844.26		844.26
12 June 20XX	GIF001/IN17	510.00		1,354.26
30 June 20XX	BACS Payment of OB and IN17		1,265.00	89.26
Balance at 30 June 20XX				89.26

Customer: Happy Engineers
Account: HAP001
Terms: 30 days

Date	Detail	Debit £	Credit £	Balance £
1 June 20XX	Opening balance	1,425.65		1,425.65
6 June 20XX	HAP001/IN24	960.00		2,385.65
22 June 20XX	BACS payment		1,425.65	960.00
26 June 20XX	HAP001/C6: IN24		186.00	774.00
28 June 20XX	HAP001/IN25	2,237.94		3,011.94
Balance at 30 June 20XX				3,011.94

Customer: Perry Cars

Account: PER001

Terms: 45 days

Date	Detail	Debit £	Credit £	Balance £
1 June 20XX	Opening balance	4,680.00		4,680.00
24 June 20XX	PER001/IN4	2,460.00		7,140.00
Balance at 30 June 20XX				7,140.00

Evidence 2a/2b

The answer provided below shows all of the information required. The candidate may upload more than one piece of evidence.

Supplier: Fabrics Delight
Account: FAB001
Terms: 60 days

Date	Detail	Debit £	Credit £	Balance £
1 June 20XX	Opening balance		1,320.11	1,320.11
16 June 20XX	Chq No:294	1,320.11		-
Balance at 30 June 20XX				NIL

Supplier: QC Exclusive
Account: QCE001
Terms: 30 days

Date	Detail	Debit £	Credit £	Balance £
1 June 20XX	Opening balance		920.46	920.46
1 June 20XX	Inv 365		1,800.00	2,720.46
Balance at 30 June 20XX				2,720.46

Supplier: Totally Wood Account: TOT001 Terms: 30 days				
Date	**Detail**	**Debit £**	**Credit £**	**Balance £**
1 June 20XX	Opening balance		135.56	135.56
12 June 20XX	PRE/14		408.00	543.56
18 June 20XX	PRE/CN3	122.40		421.16
29 June 20XX	Chq No:295	421.16		-
Balance at 30 June 20XX				NIL

Evidence 3

Audit trial

Task	Transaction Type	Account(s)	Date 20XX	Invoice/ credit note number	Net Amount £	VAT £	Allocated Against receipt/ payment	Reconciled with bank statement	Notes
1	Customer O/bal	GIF001	01 Jun		844.26		✓		
	Customer O/bal	HAP001	01 Jun		1425.65		✓		
	Customer O/bal	PER001	01 Jun		4,680.00				
2	Supplier O/bal	FAB001	01 Jun		1,320.11		✓		
	Supplier O/bal	QCE001	01 Jun		920.46		✓		
	Supplier O/bal	TOT001	01 Jun		135.56				

Task	Transaction Type	Account(s)	Date 20XX	Invoice/ credit note number	Net Amount £	VAT £	Allocated Against receipt/ payment	Reconciled with bank statement	Notes
3	Dr	Computer equipment – cost	01 Jun		4,600.00				
	Cr	Computer equipment – acc depn	01 Jun		1,200.00				
	Dr	Delivery vehicles – cost	01 Jun		22,800.00				
	Cr	Delivery vehicles – acc depn	01 Jun		5,000.00				
	Dr	Fixtures fittings – cost	01 Jun		6,445.00				
	Cr	Fixtures fittings – acc depn	01 Jun		1,625.00				
	Dr	Bank current account	01 Jun		13,984.24			✓	
	Dr	Petty cash	01 Jun		75.00				
	Cr	Sales tax control account	01 Jun		12,100.00				
	Dr	Purchases tax control account	01 Jun		7,540.00				
	Dr	Capital	01 Jun		40,093.02				
	Dr	Sales ledger control*	01 Jun		6,949.91				
	Cr	Purchases ledger control*	01 Jun		2,376.13				
		*If appropriate							

Task	Transaction Type	Account(s)		Date 20XX	Invoice/ credit note number	Net Amount £	VAT £	Allocated Against receipt/ payment	Reconciled with bank statement	Notes
4	Sales inv	HAP001	Sales – North	06 Jun	HAP001/IN24	800.00	160.00			
	Sales inv	GIF001	Sales – North	12 Jun	GIF001/IN17	425.00	85.00	✓		
	Sales inv	PER001	Sales – South	24 Jun	PER001/IN4	2,050.00	410.00			
	Sales inv	HAP001	Sales – North	28 Jun	HAP001/IN25	1,864.95	372.99			
	Sales CN	HAP001	Sales – North	26 Jun	HAP001/C6	155.00	31.00			
5	Purchases inv	QCE001	Completed units	01 Jun	365	1,500.00	300.00			
	Purchases inv	TOT001	Raw materials	12 Jun	PRE/14	340.00	68.00	✓		
	Purchases CN	TOT001	Raw materials	18 Jun	PRE/CN3	102.00	20.40	✓		

Task	Transaction Type	Account(s)		Date 20XX	Invoice/credit note number	Net Amount £	VAT £	Allocated Against receipt/payment	Reconciled with bank statement	Notes
6	Bank receipt	Bank	Online sales	09 Jun		3,546.38	709.28		✓	Accept Net and VAT amounts of + or − 1 penny for online sales due to software rounding
	Bank receipt	Bank	Online sales	16 Jun		3,211.88	642.37		✓	
	Bank receipt	Bank	Online sales	23 Jun		3,011.85	602.37		✓	
	Bank receipt	Bank	Online sales	30 Jun		1,664.16	332.83		✓	
	Bank payment	Bank	Wages	16 Jun		6,200.00			✓	
7	Customer receipt	HAP001	Bank	22 Jun		1,425.65			✓	
	Customer receipt	GIF001	Bank	30 Jun		1,265.00			✓	
8	Supplier payment	FAB001	Bank	16 Jun		1,320.11			✓	
	Supplier payment	TOT001	Bank	29 Jun		421.16	75.00		✓	
	Bank payment	Bank	Delivery expenses	30 Jun		375.00			✓	

Task	Transaction Type	Account(s)	Date 20XX	Invoice/credit note number	Net Amount £	VAT £	Allocated Against receipt/payment	Reconciled with bank statement	Notes
9	Bank payment	Bank	01 Jun		600.00			✓	
10	Cash payment	Petty cash	09 Jun		6.00	1.20			
	Cash payment	Petty cash	09 Jun		14.00				
	Cash payment	Petty cash	14 Jun		4.75				
11	Journal debit	Computer equipment – cost	30 Jun		95.00				
	Journal credit	Fixtures and fittings – cost	30 Jun		95.00				
	Journal debit	Wages	30 Jun		25.95				
	Journal credit	Bank	30 Jun		25.95			✓	
12	Bank payment	Electricity	27 Jun		101.00			✓	
	Bank payment	Bank charges	28 Jun		14.00			✓	

Evidence 4

Trial balance

Account Names	Debit Balance	Credit Balance
Computer equipment – Cost	4,695.00	
Computer equipment – Accumulated depreciation		1,200.00
Delivery vehicles – Cost	22,800.00	
Delivery vehicles – Accumulated depreciation		5,000.00
Fixtures and Fittings – Cost	6,350.00	
Fixtures and Fittings – Accumulated depreciation		1,625.00
Bank Current Account	21,263.79	
Petty cash	49.05	
Sales Ledger Control Account	10,241.20	
Purchase Ledger Control Account		2,720.46
Sales Tax Control Account		15,383.84
Purchase Tax Control Account	7,963.80	
Capital		40,093.02
Online sales		11,434.27
Sales to shops – North		2,934.95
Sales to Shops – South		2,050.00
Purchases – Completed units	1,500.00	
Purchases – Raw materials	238.00	
Wages	6,225.95	
Rent and rates	600.00	
Electricity	101.00	

BPP
LEARNING MEDIA

Account Names	Debit Balance	Credit Balance
Delivery vehicle expenses	375.00	
Bank charges	14.00	
Stationery	6.00	
Travelling	18.75	
	82,441.54	82,441.54

Evidence 5 and 6 are dependent on software used.

Additional guidance for individual tasks

If you struggled with the assessment, we suggest you read the guidance that follows and attempt the assessment again. Note that when we refer to 'Sage' in this section, this covers both Sage 50 and Sage One, unless otherwise stated.

Task 1 (3 marks)

Make sure you set up all **customers** listed and be careful to set them up as customers, rather than suppliers. Enter the dates and opening balances carefully and check that all of your entries match the information you have been given.

Note that if you are using Sage One, you need to enter the opening balance date as **31 May 20XX** as the program requires it to be one day before the accounts start date. Other programs, including Sage 50, may allow you to enter the opening balance date as 1 June 20XX.

Task 2 (3 marks)

Make sure you set up all **suppliers** listed and be careful to set them up as suppliers, rather than customers. Enter the dates and opening balances carefully and check that all of your entries match the information you have been given.

Note that if you are using Sage One, you need to enter the opening balance date as **31 May 20XX** as the program requires it to be one day before the accounts start date. Other programs, including Sage 50, may allow you to enter the opening balance date as 1 June 20XX.

Task 3 (19 marks)

Most of these accounts will already be on Sage, so you just need to enter the opening balances for these. However, for some accounts, you will need to either create new accounts or amend the names of existing accounts.

To help reduce the chance of error, be careful and methodical when entering the balances and selecting the appropriate nominal accounts. When finished, check you have not missed any accounts – you can do this by previewing a trial balance. Assuming you entered Task 1 and 2 data correctly, if you are using Sage, you will not need to enter opening balances for the sales ledger and purchase ledger control accounts.

Note that if you are using Sage One, you need to enter the opening balance date as **31 May 20XX** as the program requires it to be one day before the accounts start date. Other programs, including Sage 50, may allow you to enter the opening balance date as 1 June 20XX.

Task 4 (15 marks)

Enter the invoices and the credit note carefully, ensuring you don't enter the credit note as an invoice or vice-versa. Remember that it is very important to select the correct income account in the nominal ledger. It is clear from the invoices which type of sale each invoice relates to. Always check you have entered **all** of the transactions.

Task 5 (9 marks)

When posting purchase invoices/credit notes, make sure you select the right supplier and an appropriate nominal account. VAT should be correctly accounted for and if you select the correct tax code in Sage 50 (VAT rate in Sage One), this will be calculated automatically – all you need to do then is check it matches the VAT per the invoice. Always check you have entered **all** of the transactions.

Task 6a and 6b (9 marks)

This task requires you to process payments and receipts that are not related to credit transactions with customers or suppliers. You should use the Other Payment/Other Receipt function in Sage One or the Bank Payment/Bank Receipt function in Sage 50.

Ensure you use the right way of accounting for VAT for cash sales. You are only given the gross amount. Therefore, in Sage One, you should enter the gross amount, and the program will automatically calculate and post the VAT. In Sage 50, although it may seem odd, firstly enter the gross amount in the Net field. Then press F9 and the program will automatically calculate the net amount.

As always, the choice of nominal account is important. Depending on your software, you will probably need to create a new account or rename an existing account (as described in Task 2, Chapter 1/3). Be careful not to omit any payments or receipts.

Tasks 7 and 8 (15 marks)

When entering supplier payments or customer receipts using Sage, you should use the **Supplier Payment** or **Customer Receipt** functions (not the Bank Payment or Bank Receipt functions (Other Payment/Other Receipt functions in Sage One) as demonstrated earlier in this Text. You should find this makes it easy to allocate the payment/receipt to the correct supplier/ customer account. Don't miss out any transactions.

Task 9 (4 marks)

Recurring payments are a bit tricky in Sage 50 – when you first enter the details, they do not impact on the nominal ledger. When you go back into Recurring items in Sage 50 to process the payment, remember **you only need to process the first payment.**

For Sage One however, the process is a bit different. You create and post the first payment using the **Other Payment** function. You then go back into the payment to set up the recurrence.

Details on how to do this were covered in Chapter 2/Chapter 4 of this Text.

Note that you are required to take a screen print in this task and you can do this by pressing **Print Screen** or **PrtScn (or PrtSc)**.

In Sage One, take a screenshot of both the 'Other Payment' screen with the details of the first payment, and the 'Make Recurring' screen with details of the recurrence.

In Sage 50 take a screenshot of the Add/Edit recurring entry screen with details of the first payment and recurrence.

Task 10 (3 marks)

Remember to change the **nominal code** in Sage 50 to the **Petty Cash** ('Cash' in Sage One) nominal code when entering the payments in this task.

You can use the **Bank Transfer** function in Sage for the payment from the Bank account to the Petty cash account.

Task 11 (4 marks)

Journals should be entered carefully to ensure you debit and credit the correct accounts. Don't get the debits and credits mixed up.

Task 12 (11 marks)

Having entered the bank charges and bank interest (using the 'Other Payment' function in Sage One or the 'Bank Payment' function in Sage 50), you should reconcile the bank using the method covered in Chapter 2/Chapter 4.

In the answer provided, you can see which items you should have reconciled as they appear in the 'Matched transactions' section in the bottom half of the bank reconciliation screen in Sage 50. In Sage One, the reconciled items have a tick in 'Reconciled' column in the bank reconciliation screen.

Take a screenshot of the bank reconciliation screen just before you save the reconciliation (ie, before you click on Save button in Sage One, or the 'Reconcile' button in Sage 50).

Task 13 (5 marks)

This task tests your ability to generate the reports specified. You will get the marks available for this particular task by **generating the correct report**. You will receive these marks, even if some of the transactions within the report are incorrect, because you entered them incorrectly in earlier tasks.

There is a comprehensive section on generating reports in Chapter 2/Chapter 4 of this Text. You should look back at this if you were unable to generate and save as PDF files, any reports. **Make sure you check that you have saved all the reports.**

Specific guidance for each document/report is given below in **bold**.

Document and reports	Save/upload as:
Ensure you specify the correct date/date range for all reports:	**For the purpose of this sample assessment, save the documents to your desktop on your computer. In a real assessment you would also be required to upload these documents, but ignore the step of uploading for this sample assessment.**
A document showing all transactions with each customer during June 20XX **Run the 'Customer Activity' report. Run the 'Detailed' report in Sage 50. In Sage One, select all customers to obtain one report for all.**	File name = Evidence 1a – Name – AAT Number
A document showing the balance owed by each customer as at 30 June 20XX **Run the 'Aged Debtors Analysis – Detailed' report in Sage 50, or the 'Aged Debtors' report in Sage One and click the 'Detailed' button.**	File name = Evidence 1b – Name – AAT Number
The following information must be evidenced within these documents: • *Customer name* • *Account code* • *Payment terms* **You need a separate document for payment terms – a screenshot of the Customer Record screen for each customer in Sage One. For Sage 50, you need the Credit Control screen within each Customer Record.**	Depending on your software you may need to save one or more documents. **Name these in the same way as above, continuing the sequence, eg, Evidence 1c...**

Document and reports	Save/upload as:
A document showing all transactions with each supplier during June 20XX **Run the 'Supplier Activity' report. Run the 'Detailed' report in Sage 50. In Sage One, select all suppliers to obtain one report for all.**	File name = **Evidence 2a – Name – AAT Number**
A document showing the balance owed to each supplier as at 30 June 20XX **Run the 'Aged Creditors Analysis – Detailed' report in Sage 50, or the 'Aged Creditors' report in Sage One and click the 'Detailed' button.**	File name = Evidence 2b – Name – AAT Number
The following information must be evidenced within these documents: • *Supplier name* • *Account code* • *Payment terms* You need a separate document for payment terms – a screenshot of the Supplier Record screen for each supplier in Sage One. For Sage 50, you need the Credit Control screen within each Supplier Record)	Depending on your software you may need to save one or more documents.
Audit trail, showing full details of all transactions, including details of receipts/payments allocated to items in customer/supplier accounts and details in the bank account that have been reconciled **Run the 'Audit Trail – Detailed' report.** **To show bank reconciled items:** **Sage 50 - reconciled items have an 'R' in the 'B' column of the report.**	File name = **Evidence 3 – Name – AAT Number**

Document and reports	Save/upload as:
Sage One - ensure the report is configured to include 'Bank Reconciled' column. Reconciled items have a tick in this column. **To show receipts/payments allocated to items in customer/supplier accounts:** *Sage 50 - the report indicates the invoices that receipts/payments are allocated to, eg, '24.42 to PI 4' shows that a payment of 24.42 is allocated to purchase invoice no. 4.* *Sage One - use the Customer/Supplier Activity reports generated in 1a and 2a above. Allocated items are identified by having 0.00 in the 'Outstanding' column)*	
Trial Balance as at 30 June 20XX **Run the 'Trial balance' report**	File name = **Evidence 4 – Name – AAT Number**
A screenshot of the recurring entry screen including all relevant input details. **From Task 9b** **In Sage One, take a screenshot of both the 'Other Payment' screen with the details of the first payment, and the 'Create Recurring Payment' screen with details of the recurrence.** **In Sage 50 take a screenshot of the Add/Edit recurring entry screen with details of the first payment and recurrence.**	File name = **Evidence 5 – Name – AAT Number**

Document and reports	Save/upload as:
A screenshot of the bank reconciliation screen showing the reconciled items. **From Task 12b** **Take a screenshot of the bank reconciliation screen just before you save the reconciliation (ie, before you click on Save button in Sage One and Reconcile button in Sage 50)**	File name = **Evidence 6 – Name – AAT Number**

BPP PRACTICE ASSESSMENT 1
Using Accounting Software

Time allowed: 2 hours

- You are now ready to attempt the BPP practice assessment for Using Accounting Software.

- This practice assessment uses a standard rate of VAT of 20%.

- It requires you to input data into a computerised accounting package and produce documents and reports.

- Ensure your accounting software is correctly set up before starting the assessment

- Answers are provided at the end of the assessment.

Using Accounting Software
BPP practice assessment 1

Assessment information (taken from AAT Sample Assessment)

The time allowed to complete this assessment is **2 hours.**

This assessment consists of **13 tasks** and it is important that you attempt them all.

- You will be asked to produce documents and reports to demonstrate your competence.

- You must then upload these documents so they can be marked by AAT.

All documents must be uploaded within the **total time** available. It is important that you upload **all** reports and documents specified in the tasks so your work can be assessed.

You will be able to attach and remove files throughout the duration of this assessment until you click on 'Finish', which will submit your assessment.

All uploaded documents should be saved and titled with the following information:

- Evidence number
- Your name
- Your AAT membership number

The evidence number to use for each document is stated in the table in Task 13.

Example

Your name is Simon White, and your AAT membership number is: 12345678

Evidence 1

A document showing all of the purchase invoices and credit notes (by purchase type) posted in January 20XX.

This document would be saved and uploaded as: Evidence 1 – Simon White – 12345678

If multiple documents are uploaded to show competency in an individual task, name these Evidence 1A and Evidence 1B and so on.

Unless the assessment asks for a specific format, you can choose the format which will best enable the marker to review and assess your work.

During the assessment, you will only make entries to the nominal ledger accounts you created in Task 3. You will not be required to make any entries to any accounts other than those you have already created.

Information

This assessment is based on an existing business, **Steadman Computer Solutions (SCS)**, a UK business that supplies computers to local businesses. It also offers a computer repair service. The owner of the business is **James Steadman,** who operates as a sole trader. James is changing from a manual book-keeping system to a computerised one from **1 January 20XX**. You are employed as an accounting technician.

Information relating to the business:

Business name:	Steadman Computer Solutions
Business address:	50 George Street Cheltenham GL50 1XR
Business owner:	James Steadman
Accounting period end:	31 December (each year)
VAT Number:	123456789 (standard scheme)
VAT rate:	Standard rate VAT of 20% charged on all sales

Sales

James likes to keep a record of the different sales made by the business, by sales type:

- Desktop computers
- Laptop computers
- Computer repairs

You have been asked to carry out the bookkeeping tasks for January 20XX **only**, the first month that the business will be using computerised accounting software and the start of the new accounting period.

All documents have been checked for accuracy and have been authorised by James Steadman.

Before you start the assessment you should:

- Set the system software date as **31st January of the current year**.
- Set the financial year to start on **1st January of the current year**.

Task 1

Refer to the customer listing below and set up customer records to open sales ledger accounts for each customer, entering opening balances at 1 January 20XX.

Customer Listing

CUSTOMER NAME, ADDRESS AND CONTACT DETAILS	CUSTOMER ACCOUNT CODE	CUSTOMER ACCOUNT DETAILS AT 1 JANUARY 20XX
Always Insurance plc 26 High Road Cheltenham GL52 8KK	ALW01	Payment terms: 30 days Opening balance: £1,821.70
Local Bank Ltd 56 Long Lane Gloucester GL10 8BN	LOC01	Payment terms: 30 days Opening balance: £1,300.00
Large Firm LLP 1 Main Road Swindon SN3 1PP	LAR01	Payment terms: 30 days Opening balance: £800.80

Task 2

Refer to the supplier listing below and set up supplier records to open purchases ledger accounts for each supplier, entering opening balances at 1 January 20XX.

Supplier Listing

SUPPLIER NAME, ADDRESS AND CONTACT DETAILS	SUPPLIER ACCOUNT CODE	SUPPLIER ACCOUNT DETAILS AT 1 JANUARY 20XX
Bell Computers Ltd 15 Queen Street London W12 9ZZ	BEL01	Payment terms: 30 days Opening balance: £1,400.00
Discount IT Supplies 50 Banner Place Gloucester GL10 4GG	DIS01	Payment terms: 30 days Opening balance: £790.40
Anderson Garages 19 Anderson Road Cheltenham GL51 5JR	AND01	Payment terms: 30 days Opening balance: £178.80

Task 3

Refer to the list of nominal ledger balances below:

Set up nominal ledger records for each account, entering opening balances (if applicable) at 1 January 20XX, ensuring you select, amend or create appropriate nominal ledger account codes.

Opening Trial Balance as at 01.01.20XX

ACCOUNT NAMES	Debit balance £	Credit balance £
Office Equipment	3,567.00	
Motor Vehicles	12,750.00	
Bank	3101.80	
Petty Cash	200.00	
Sales ledger control* (see note below)	3,922.50	
Purchases ledger control* (see note below)		2,369.20
Sales tax control account		1,540.60
Purchase tax control account	1,080.20	
Capital		20,000.00
Drawings	4,660.10	
Sales – Desktops		8,780.00
Sales – Laptops		5,920.00
Sales – Computer repairs		620.80
Computers for resale – purchases	8,880.20	
Rent and rates	810.00	
Bank interest paid	NIL	
Bank charges	NIL	
Motor vehicle expenses	258.80	
	39,230.60	**39,230.60**

* **Note.** As you have already entered opening balances for customers and suppliers, the software package you are using may not require you to enter these balances.

In the rest of the assessment, you will only make entries to the nominal ledger accounts you created in Task 3. You will not be required to make any entries to any accounts other than those you have already created.

Task 4

Refer to the following summary of purchase invoices and purchase credit notes and enter these transactions into the accounting software, ensuring you enter all the information below and select the correct purchases code.

Summary of purchase invoices

Date 20XX	Supplier Name	Invoice Number	Gross £	VAT £	Net £	Computers for resale £	Moto expen £
03.01.XX	Bell Computers	SC2040	2,520.00	420.00	2,100.00	2,100.00	
09.01.XX	Anderson Garages	R2168	192.00	32.00	160.00		16(
21.01.XX	Discount IT Supplies	1806	2,493.60	415.60	2,078.00	2,078.00	
28.01.XX	Bell Computers	SC2349	600.00	100.00	500.00	500.00	
	Totals		**5,805.60**	**967.60**	**4,838.00**	**4,678.00**	**16(**

Summary of purchase credit notes

Date 20XX	Supplier Name	Invoice Number	Gross £	VAT £	Net £	Computers for resale £	Moto expen £
23.01.XX	Bell Computers	CR0358*	480.00	80.00	400.00	400.00	
	Totals		**480.00**	**80.00**	**400.00**	**400.00**	

* The credit note relates to some items on invoice SC2040.

Task 5

Refer to the following sales invoices and sales credit notes and enter these transactions into the accounting software, ensuring you enter all the information below and select the correct sales code.

Steadman Computer Solutions
50 George Street, Cheltenham, GL50 1XR
VAT Registration No 478 3164 00

Telephone: 01242 866 5128
Email: J.Steadman@SCS.co.uk

SALES INVOICE NO 0100

Date: 01 January 20XX

Local Bank Ltd
56 Long Lane
Gloucester
GL10 8BN

	£
2 new laptops	800.00
VAT @ 20%	160.00
Total for payment	960.00
Terms: 30 days	

Steadman Computer Solutions
50 George Street, Cheltenham, GL50 1XR
VAT Registration No 478 3164 00

Telephone: 01242 866 5128
Email: J.Steadman@SCS.co.uk

SALES INVOICE NO 0101

Date: 15 January 20XX

Large Firm LLP
1 Main Road
Swindon
SN3 1PP

	£
5 new desktop PCs	2,520.50
VAT @ 20%	504.10
Total for payment	3,024.60
Terms: 30 days	

Steadman Computer Solutions
50 George Street, Cheltenham, GL50 1XR
VAT Registration No 478 3164 00

Telephone: 01242 866 5128
Email: J.Steadman@SCS.co.uk

S A L E S   CREDIT NOTE N O   0020
Linked to INVOICE NO 0100
Date: 18 January 20XX

Local Bank Ltd
56 Long Lane
Gloucester
GL10 8BN

	£
Return of unwanted laptop	400.00
VAT @ 20%	80.00
Total for payment	480.00
Terms: 30 days	

Task 6a

Refer to the following receipt issued for cash sales and enter these transactions into the accounting software.

Date	Payment method	Details	Amount
7 January 20XX	Cheque	Minor repair to a laptop computer	£60.00 including VAT
15 January 20XX	Cash	Repair to desktop PC computer	£120.00 including VAT
23 January 20XX	Cheque	Sales of used laptop computer	£200.00 including VAT
27 January 20XX	Cash	Sale of used desktop PC computer	£150.00 including VAT

Task 6b

Refer to the following email below from James Steadman and enter this transaction into the accounting software.

Email	
From:	James Steadman
To:	Accounting Technician
Date:	12 January 20XX
Subject:	Drawings

Hello

I have withdrawn £180 in cash from the business bank for my personal use.

Please record this transaction.

Thanks

James

Task 7

Refer to the following summary of payments received from customers and enter these transactions into the accounting software, making sure you allocate all amounts, as shown in the details column.

Receipts listing

Date	Receipt type	Customer	£	Details
14.01.XX	BACS	Always Insurance plc	1,821.70	Payment of opening balance
28.01.XX	Faster Payment	Local Bank Ltd	480.00	Payment of invoice 0100 including credit note 0020

Task 8

Refer to the following summary of payments made to suppliers and enter these transactions into the accounting software, making sure you allocate (where applicable) all amounts, as shown in the details column.

Cheques paid listing

Date	Cheque number	Supplier	£	Details
11.01.XX	003241	Bell Computers Ltd	1,000.00	Payment on account
20.01.XX	003242	Anderson Garages	192.00	Payment of invoice R2168
23.01.XX	003243	Discount IT Supplies	790.40	Payment of opening balance

Task 9

Refer to the following direct debit details:

(a) Set up a recurring entry, as shown in the table below.

(b) Save a screen shot of the screen, setting up the recurring entry prior to processing. You will be provided with the required evidence number for this in Task 13.

(c) Process the first payment.

Direct debit details

Details	Amount	First payment	Number of monthly payments
Rates (VAT not applicable)	£300	24 January 20XX	12

Task 10

(a) **Refer to the following petty cash vouchers and enter the petty cash payments into the accounting software.**

Petty Cash Voucher	
Date 16 January 20XX	**No** PC042
	£
Train ticket for business travel – VAT not applicable	38.00
Receipt attached	

Petty Cash Voucher	
Date 20 January 20XX	**No** PC043
	£
A4 pads, folders and ball point pens	31.60
VAT	6.32
Total	37.92
Receipt attached	

(b) **Refer to the following petty cash reimbursement slip and enter this transaction into the accounting software.**

Petty Cash Reimbursement PCR No 03	
Date: 31 January 20XX	
Cash from the bank account to restore the petty cash account to £200.00.	£75.92

Task 11

Refer to the following journal entries and enter them into the accounting software.

JOURNAL ENTRIES TO BE MADE 15.01.XX	£	£
Drawings	85.00	
Motor expenses		85.00
Being journal to reflect personal motor expenses posted as business expenses		

JOURNAL ENTRIES TO BE MADE 30.01.XX	£	£
Sales - Desktops	400.00	
Sales - Laptops		400.00
Being correction of an error in where a Laptop sale was originally incorrectly recorded as a Desktop sale		

Task 12

Refer to the following bank statement. Using the accounting software and the transactions you have already posted:

(a) Enter any additional items on the bank statement that have yet to be recorded, into the accounting software (ignore VAT on any of these transactions).

(b) Reconcile the bank statement. If the bank statement does not reconcile, check your work and make the necessary corrections.

(c) Save a screenshot of the bank reconciliation screen. You will be provided with the required evidence number for this in Task 13.

South Bank plc
60 Broad Street
Cheltenham
GL51 9YY

Steadman Computer Solutions
50 George Street
Cheltenham
GL50 1XR
Account number 00698435

31 January 20XX

STATEMENT OF ACCOUNT

Date 20XX	Details	Paid out £	Paid in £	Balance £
01 Jan	Opening balance			3,101.80C
09 Jan	Counter credit		60.00	3,161.80C
12 Jan	Cash withdrawal	180.00		2,981.80C
14 Jan	BACS: Always Insurance plc		1,821.70	4,803.50C
14 Jan	Cheque 003241	1,000.00		3,803.50C
17 Jan	Counter credit		120.00	3,923.50C
24 Jan	Cheque 003242	192.00		3,731.50C
24 Jan	Direct Debit – Cheltenham MBC – Rates	300.00		3,431.50C
25 Jan	Counter credit		200.00	3,631.50C
27 Jan	Counter credit		150.00	3,781.50C
28 Jan	Faster payment: Local Bank Ltd		480.00	4,261.50C
29 Jan	Cheque 003243	790.40		3,471.10C
30 Jan	Bank charges	12.40		3,458.70C
31 Jan	Bank interest	1.14		3,457.56C
31 Jan	Transfer	75.92		3,381.64C
	D = Debit C = Credit			

Task 13

Documentation of evidence

You are now required to generate the following documents to demonstrate your competence:

Document and reports	Save / upload as:
A document showing all transactions with each customer during January 20XX	File name = Evidence 1a – Name – AAT Number
A document showing the balance owed by each customer as at 31 January 20XX *The following information must be evidenced within these documents:* • Customer name • Account code • Payment terms	File name = Evidence 1b – Name – AAT Number Depending on your software you may need to save one or more documents.
A document showing all transactions with each supplier during January 20XX	File name = Evidence 2a – Name – AAT Number
A document showing the balance owed to each supplier as at 31 January 20XX *The following information must be evidenced within these documents:* • Supplier name • Account code • Payment terms	File name = Evidence 2b – Name – AAT Number Depending on your software you may need to save one or more documents.
Audit trail, showing full details of all transactions, including details of receipts/ payments allocated to items in customer/ supplier accounts and details in the bank account that have been reconciled.	File name = Evidence 3 – Name – AAT Number
Trial Balance as at 31 January 20XX	File name = Evidence 4 – Name – AAT Number
A screenshot of the recurring entry screen including all relevant input details.	File name = Evidence 5 – Name – AAT Number
A screenshot of the bank reconciliation screen showing the reconciled items.	File name = Evidence 6 – Name – AAT Number

BPP PRACTICE ASSESSMENT 1
Using Accounting Software

ANSWERS

Using Accounting Software
BPP practice assessment 1

Some answers are given below. The answers we've provided are indicative of relevant content within the audit trail, the exact format of which will differ according to the computerised accounting package used.

Task	Transaction type	Account(s)	Date 20XX	Net Amount £	VAT £	Allocated against receipt/ payment ✓	Reconciled with bank statement ✓
1	Customer O/bal	ALW01	01 Jan	1,821.70		✓	
	Customer O/bal	LOC01	01 Jan	1,300.00			
	Customer O/bal	LAR01	01 Jan	800.80			
2	Supplier O/bal	BEL01	01 Jan	1,400.00			
	Supplier O/bal	DIS01	01 Jan	790.40		✓	
	Supplier O/bal	AND01	01 Jan	178.80			
3	Debit	Office equipment	01 Jan	3,567.00			
	Debit	Motor vehicles	01 Jan	12,750.00			
	Debit	Bank current account	01 Jan	3,101.80			✓
	Debit	Petty cash	01 Jan	200.00			
	Debit	Sales ledger control	01 Jan	3,922.50			
	Credit	Purchases ledger control	01 Jan	2,369.20			
	Credit	VAT on sales	01 Jan	1,540.60			
	Debit	VAT on purchases	01 Jan	1,080.20			
	Credit	Capital	01 Jan	20,000.00			
	Debit	Drawings	01 Jan	4,660.10			
	Credit	Sales – Desktops	01 Jan	8,780,00.00			
	Credit	Sales – Laptops	01 Jan	5,920.00			
	Credit	Sales – Computer repairs	01 Jan	620.80			
	Debit	Computers for re-sale – purchases	01 Jan	8,880.20			
	Debit	Rent and rates	01 Jan	810.00			
	Debit	Motor vehicle expenses	01 Jan	258.80			

Task	Transaction type	Account(s)		Date 20XX	Net Amount £	VAT £	Allocated against receipt/ payment ✓	Reconciled with bank statement ✓
4	Purchases inv	BEL01	Computers for re-sale	03 Jan	2,100.00	420.00		
	Purchases inv	AND0	Motor vehicle expenses	09 Jan	160.00	32.00	✓	
	Purchases inv	DIS01	Computers for re-sale	21 Jan	2078.00	415.60		
	Purchases inv	BEL01	Computers for re-sale	28 Jan	500.00	100.00		
	Purchases Cr	BEL01	Computers for re-sale	23 Jan	400.00	80.00		
5	Sales inv	LOC01	Sales – Laptops	01 Jan	800.00	160.00	✓	
	Sales inv	LAR01	Sales – Desktops	15 Jan	2,520.50	504.10		
	Sales CN	LOC01		18 Jan	400.00	80.00	✓	
6a	Bank receipt (Other receipt in Sage One)	Bank	Sales – Computer repairs	07 Jan	50.00	10.00		✓
	Bank/Other receipt	Bank	Sales – Computer repairs	15 Jan	100.00	20.00		✓
	Bank/Other receipt	Bank	Sales – Laptops	23 Jan	166.67	33.33		✓
	Bank/Other receipt	Bank	Sales – Desktop	28 Jan	125.00	25.00		✓
6b	Bank payment	Bank	Drawings	12 Jan	180.00			✓
7	Customer receipt	ALW01	Bank	14 Jan	1,821.70			✓
	Customer receipt	LOC01	Bank	26 Jan	480.00			✓
8	Supplier payment on a/c	BEL01	Bank	11 Jan	1,000.00			✓
	Supplier payment	AND01	Bank	20 Jan	192.00			✓
	Supplier payment	DIS01	Bank	23 Jan	790.40			✓

Task	Transaction type	Account(s)		Date 20XX	Net Amount £	VAT £	Allocated against receipt/ payment ✓	Reconciled with bank statement ✓
9	Bank payment	Bank	Rates – DD	24 Jan	300.00			✓
10	Cash payment	Petty cash	Travel	16 Jan	38.00			
	Cash payment	Petty cash	Stationery	20 Jan	31.60	6.32		
	Debit	Petty cash		31 Jan	75.92			
	Credit	Bank		31 Jan	75.92			✓
11	Journal debit	Drawings		15 Jan	85.00			
	Journal credit	Motor expenses		15 Jan	85.00			
	Journal debit	Sales – Desktops		30 Jan	400.00			
	Journal credit	Sales – Laptops		30 Jan	400.00			
12	Bank payment (Other payment in Sage One)	Bank	Bank charges and interest (Sage One) or Bank charges (Sage 50)	30 Jan	12.40			✓
	Bank / Other payment	Bank	Bank charges and interest (Sage One) or Bank interest paid (Sage 50)	31 Jan	1.14			✓

Additional guidance for individual tasks

If you struggled with the assessment, we suggest you read the guidance that follows and attempt the assessment again. Note that when we refer to 'Sage' in this section, this covers both Sage 50 and Sage One, unless otherwise stated.

Task 1 (guidance)

Make sure you set up all **customers** listed and be careful to set them up as customers, rather than suppliers. Enter the dates and opening balances carefully and check that all of your entries match the information you have been given.

Note that if you are using Sage One, you need to enter the opening balance date as **31 December 20XW** as the program requires it to be one day before the accounts start date. Other programs, including Sage 50, may allow you to enter the opening balance date as 1 January 20XX.

Task 2 (guidance)

Make sure you set up all **suppliers** listed and be careful to set them up as suppliers, rather than customers. Enter the dates and opening balances carefully and check that all of your entries match the information you have been given.

Note that if you are using Sage One, you need to enter the opening balance date as **31 December 20XW** as the program requires it to be one day before the accounts start date. Other programs, including Sage 50, may allow you to enter the opening balance date as 1 January 20XX.

Task 3 (guidance)

Most of these accounts will already be on Sage, so you just need to enter the opening balances for these. However, for some accounts, you will need to either create new accounts or amend the names of existing accounts.

To help reduce the chance of error, be careful and methodical when entering the balances and selecting the appropriate nominal accounts. When finished, check you have not missed any accounts – you can do this by previewing a trial balance. Assuming you entered Task 1 and 2 data correctly, if you are using Sage, you will not need to enter opening balances for the sales ledger and purchase ledger control accounts.

Note that if you are using Sage One, you need to enter the opening balance date as **31 December 20XW** as the program requires it to be one day before the accounts start date. Other programs, including Sage 50, may allow you to enter the opening balance date as 1 January 20XX.

Task 4 (guidance)

When posting purchase invoices/credit notes, make sure you select the right supplier and an appropriate nominal account. VAT should be correctly accounted for and if you set the correct tax code in Sage 50 (VAT rate in Sage One), this will be calculated automatically – all you need to do then is check it matches the VAT shown on the invoice. Always check you have entered **all** of the transactions.

Task 5 (guidance)

Enter the invoices and the credit note carefully, ensuring you don't enter the credit note as an invoice or vice-versa. Remember that it is very important to select the correct income account in the nominal ledger. It is clear from the invoices which type of sale each invoice relates to. Always check you have entered **all** of the transactions.

Task 6a and 6b (guidance)

This task requires you to process payments and receipts that are not related to credit transactions with customers or suppliers. You should use the Other Payment/Other Receipt function in Sage One or the Bank Payment/Bank Receipt function in Sage 50.

Ensure you use the right way of accounting for VAT for cash sales. You are only given the gross amount. Therefore, in Sage One, you should enter the gross amount, and the program will automatically calculate and post the VAT. In Sage 50, although it may seem odd, firstly enter the gross amount in the Net field. Then press F9 and the program will automatically calculate the net amount.

As always, the choice of nominal account is important. Be careful not to omit any payments or receipts.

Tasks 7 and 8 (guidance)

When entering supplier payments or customer receipts using Sage, you should use the **Supplier Payment** or **Customer Receipt** functions (not the Bank Payment or Bank Receipt functions (Other Payment/Other Receipt functions in Sage One) as demonstrated earlier in this Text. You should find this makes it easy to allocate the payment/receipt to the correct supplier/ customer account. Don't miss out any transactions.

Task 9 (guidance)

Recurring payments are a bit tricky in Sage 50 – when you first enter the details, they do not impact on the nominal ledger. When you go back into Recurring items in Sage 50 to process the payment, remember **you only need to process the first payment.**

For Sage One however, the process is a bit different. You create and post the first payment using the **Other Payment** function. You then go back into the payment to set up the recurrence.

Details on how to do this were covered in Chapter 2/Chapter 4 of this Text.

Note that you are required to take a screen print in this task and you can do this by pressing **Print Screen** or **PrtScn (or PrtSc)**.

In Sage One, take a screenshot of both the 'Other Payment' screen with the details of the first payment, and the 'Make Recurring' screen with details of the recurrence.

In Sage 50 take a screenshot of the Add/Edit recurring entry screen with details of the first payment and recurrence.

Task 10 (guidance)

Remember to change the **nominal code** in Sage 50 to the **Petty Cash** ('Cash' in Sage One) nominal code when entering the payments in this task.

You can use the **Bank Transfer** function in Sage for the payment from the Bank account to the Petty cash account.

Task 11 (guidance)

Journals should be entered carefully to ensure you debit and credit the correct accounts. Don't get the debits and credits mixed up.

Task 12 (guidance)

Having entered the bank charges and bank interest (using the 'Other Payment' function in Sage One or the 'Bank Payment' function in Sage 50), you should reconcile the bank using the method covered in Chapter 2/Chapter 4.

In the answer provided, you can see which items you should have reconciled as they appear in the 'Matched transactions' section in the bottom half of the bank reconciliation screen in Sage 50. In Sage One, the reconciled items have a tick in 'Reconciled' column in the bank reconciliation screen.

Take a screenshot of the bank reconciliation screen just before you save the reconciliation (ie, before you click on Save button in Sage One, or the 'Reconcile' button in Sage 50).

Task 13 (guidance)

This task tests your ability to generate the reports specified. You will get the marks available for this particular task by **generating the correct report**. You will receive these marks, even if some of the transactions within the report are incorrect, because you entered them incorrectly in earlier tasks.

There is a comprehensive section on generating reports in Chapter 2/Chapter 4 of this Text. You should look back at this if you were unable to generate and save as PDF files, any reports. **Make sure you check that you have saved all the reports.**

Specific guidance for each document/report is given below in **bold**.

Document and reports	Save / upload as:
Ensure you specify the correct date/date range for all reports:	**For the purpose of this practice assessment, save the documents to your desktop on your computer. In a real assessment you would also be required to upload these documents, but ignore the step of uploading for this practice assessment.**
A document showing all transactions with each customer during January 20XX **Run the 'Customer Activity' report. Run the 'Detailed' report in Sage 50. In Sage One, select all customers to obtain one report for all.**	File name = Evidence 1a – Name – AAT Number
A document showing the balance owed by each customer as at 31 January 20XX **Run the 'Aged Debtors Analysis – Detailed' report in Sage 50, or the 'Aged Debtors' report in Sage One and click the 'Detailed' button.**	File name = Evidence 1b – Name – AAT Number

Document and reports	Save / upload as:
The following information must be evidenced within these documents: • Customer name • Account code • Payment terms **You need a separate document for payment terms – a screenshot of the Customer Record screen for each customer in Sage One. For Sage 50, you need the Credit Control screen within each Customer Record.**	Depending on your software you may need to save one or more documents. **Name these in the same way as above, continuing the sequence, eg, Evidence 1c...**
A document showing all transactions with each supplier during January 20XX **Run the 'Supplier Activity' report. Run the 'Detailed' report in Sage 50. In Sage One, select all suppliers to obtain one report for all.**	File name = **Evidence 2a – Name – AAT Number**
A document showing the balance owed to each supplier as at 31 January 20XX **Run the 'Aged Creditors Analysis – Detailed' report in Sage 50, or the 'Aged Creditors' report in Sage One and click the 'Detailed' button.**	File name = Evidence 2b – Name – AAT Number
The following information must be evidenced within these documents: • Supplier name • Account code • Payment terms You need a separate document for payment terms – a screenshot of the Supplier Record screen for each supplier in Sage One. For Sage 50, you need the Credit Control screen within each Supplier Record)	Depending on your software you may need to save one or more documents.

Document and reports	Save / upload as:
Audit trail, showing full details of all transactions, including details of receipts/payments allocated to items in customer/supplier accounts and details in the bank account that have been reconciled **Run the 'Audit Trail – Detailed' report.** **To show bank reconciled items:** *Sage 50 - reconciled items have an 'R' in the 'B' column of the report.* *Sage One - ensure the report is configured to include 'Bank Reconciled' column. Reconciled items have a tick in this column.* **To show receipts/payments allocated to items in customer/supplier accounts:** *Sage 50 - the report indicates the invoices that receipts/payments are allocated to, eg, '24.42 to PI 4' shows that a payment of 24.42 is allocated to purchase invoice no. 4.* *Sage One - use the Customer/Supplier Activity reports generated in 1a and 2a above. Allocated items are identified by having 0.00 in the 'Outstanding' column)*	File name = **Evidence 3 – Name – AAT Number**
Trial Balance as at 31 January 20XX **Run the 'Trial balance' report**	File name = **Evidence 4 – Name – AAT Number**

Document and reports	Save / upload as:
A screenshot of the recurring entry screen including all relevant input details. **From Task 9b** **In Sage One, take a screenshot of both the 'Other Payment' screen with the details of the first payment, and the 'Create Recurring Payment' screen with details of the recurrence.** **In Sage 50 take a screenshot of the Add/Edit recurring entry screen with details of the first payment and recurrence.**	File name = **Evidence 5 – Name – AAT Number**
A screenshot of the bank reconciliation screen showing the reconciled items. **From Task 12b** **Take a screenshot of the bank reconciliation screen just before you save the reconciliation (ie, before you click on Save button in Sage One and Reconcile button in Sage 50)**	File name = **Evidence 6 – Name – AAT Number**

BPP PRACTICE ASSESSMENT 2
Using Accounting Software

Time allowed: 2 hours

- You are now ready to attempt the BPP practice assessment for Using Accounting Software.

- This practice assessment uses a standard rate of VAT of 20%.

- It requires you to input data into a computerised accounting package and produce documents and reports.

- Ensure your accounting software is correctly set up before starting the assessment

- Answers are provided at the end of the assessment.

Using Accounting Software
BPP practice assessment 2

This is the old AQ2013 AAT sample assessment, adapted for the AQ2016 syllabus.

Assessment information (taken from AAT Sample Assessment)

The time allowed to complete this assessment is **2 hours.**

This assessment consists of **13 tasks** and it is important that you attempt them all.

- You will be asked to produce documents and reports to demonstrate your competence.

- You must then upload these documents so they can be marked by AAT.

All documents must be uploaded within the **total time** available. It is important that you upload **all** reports and documents specified in the tasks so your work can be assessed.

You will be able to attach and remove files throughout the duration of this assessment until you click on 'Finish', which will submit your assessment.

All uploaded documents should be saved and titled with the following information:

- Evidence number
- Your name
- Your AAT membership number

The evidence number to use for each document is stated in the table in Task 13.

Example

Your name is Simon White, and your AAT membership number is: 12345678

Evidence 1

A document showing all of the purchase invoices and credit notes (by purchase type) posted in May 20XX.

This document would be saved and uploaded as: Evidence 1 – Simon White – 12345678

If multiple documents are uploaded to show competency in an individual task, name these Evidence 1A and Evidence 1B and so on.

Unless the assessment asks for a specific format, you can choose the format which will best enable the marker to review and assess your work.

During the assessment, you will only make entries to the nominal ledger accounts you created in Task 3. You will not be required to make any entries to any accounts other than those you have already created.

Information

This assessment is based on an existing business, **Campbell Kitchens**, an organisation that supplies kitchen furniture and equipment. The owner of the business is **Kitty Campbell** who operates as a sole trader. At the start of business, Kitty operated a manual bookkeeping system but has now decided that from **1 May 20XX** the accounting system will become computerised. You are employed as an accounting technician

Information relating to the business:

Business name:	Campbell Kitchens
Business address:	47 Landsway Road Stotton ST4 9TX
Business owner:	Kitty Campbell
Accounting period end:	30 April (each year)
VAT Number:	123456789 (standard scheme)
VAT rate:	Standard rate VAT of 20% charged on all sales

Sales

Kitty likes to keep a record of the different sales made by the business, by sales type:

- Kitchen furniture
- Kitchen equipment

You have been asked to carry out the bookkeeping tasks for May 20XX **only**, the first month that the business will be using computerised accounting software and the start of the new accounting period.

All documents have been checked for accuracy and have been authorised by Kitty Campbell.

Before you start the assessment you should:

- Set the system software date as **31 May of the current year**
- Set the financial year to start on **1 May of the current year**

Task 1

Refer to the customer listing below and set up customer records to open sales ledger accounts for each customer, entering opening balances at 1 May 20XX.

Customer Listing

CUSTOMER NAME AND ADDRESS	CUSTOMER ACCOUNT CODE	CUSTOMER ACCOUNT DETAILS AT 1 MAY 20XX
Fraser Designs 291 Tower Way Stotton ST7 4PQ	FRA001	Payment terms: 30 days Opening balance: £2,017.60
Fry and Partners 9 Carters Lane Brigtown BG1 3QT	FRY002	Payment terms: 30 days Opening balance: £1,597.60
SCL Interiors 14 Dingle Street Stotton ST4 2LY	SCL001	Payment terms: 30 days Opening balance: £1,906.50

Task 2

Refer to the supplier listing below and set up supplier records to open purchases ledger accounts for each supplier, entering opening balances at 1 May 20XX.

Supplier Listing

SUPPLIER NAME AND ADDRESS	SUPPLIER ACCOUNT CODE	SUPPLIER ACCOUNT DETAILS AT 1 MAY 20XX
Hart Ltd 3 Lion Street Stotton ST8 2HX	HAR001	Payment terms: 30 days Opening balance: £1,012.75
Jackson Builders 75 Stevens Street Brigtown BG5 3PE	JAC001	Payment terms: 30 days Opening balance: £456.35
Vanstone plc 404 Larchway Estate Brigtown BG9 7HJ	VAN001	Payment terms: 30 days Opening balance: £2,097.40

Task 3

Refer to the list of **nominal ledger accounts** below:

Set up nominal ledger records for each account, entering opening balances (if applicable) at 1 May 20XX, ensuring you select, amend or create appropriate nominal ledger account codes.

Opening Trial Balance as at 01 May 20XX

ACCOUNT NAMES	Debit balance £	Credit balance £
Motor Vehicles	20,067.10	
Bank current account	4,916.26	
Petty Cash	68.24	
Sales tax control account		1,497.68
Purchase tax control account	909.23	
Capital		26,416.85
Drawings	350.00	
Sales – kitchen furniture		456.20
Sales – kitchen equipment		119.30
Goods for re-sale	224.00	
Sales ledger control* (see note below)	5,521.70	
Purchases ledger control* (see note below)		3,566.50
Bank interest received		NIL
Bank charges	NIL	
	32,056.53	**32,056.53**

* Note. As you have already entered opening balances for customers and suppliers, the software package you are using may not require you to enter these balances.

In the rest of the assessment, you will only make entries to the nominal ledger accounts you created in Task 3. You will not be required to make any entries to any accounts other than those you have already created.

••

Task 4

Refer to the following summary of sales invoices and summary of sales credit notes and enter these transactions into the accounting software, ensuring you enter all the information below and select the correct sales account code.

Summary of sales invoices

Date 20XX	Customer name	Invoice number	Gross £	VAT £	Net £	Kitchen furniture £	Kitchen equipment £
7 May	Fry and Partners	523	2,011.68	335.28	1,676.40	1,676.40	
21 May	Fraser Designs	524	852.24	142.04	710.20		710.2
23 May	SCL Interiors	525	1,499.00	249.83	1,249.17	1,249.17	
27 May	Fry and Partners	526	535.40	89.23	446.17	446.17	
	Totals		4,898.32	816.38	4,081.94	3,371.74	710.

Summary of sales credit notes

Date 20XX	Customer name	Credit note number	Gross £	VAT £	Net £	Kitchen furniture £	Kitchen equipment £
14 May	Fry and Partners	61*	500.16	83.36	416.80	416.80	
	Totals		500.16	83.36	416.80	416.80	0

* The credit note relates to some items that make up the opening balance of Fry and Partners at 1 May 20XX.

Task 5

Refer to the following purchase invoices and the purchases credit note and enter these transactions into the accounting software, ensuring you enter all the information below and select the correct purchases code.

Purchase invoices

Jackson Builders

75 Steven Street, Brigtown, BG5 3PE

VAT Registration No 321 3726 89

INVOICE NO 5/219

Date: 12 May 20XX

Campbell Kitchens
47 Landsway Road
Stotton
ST4 9TX

	£
Repairs to building	909.25
VAT @ 20%	181.85
Total for payment	1,091.10

Terms: 30 days

Vanstone plc
404 Larchway Estate, Brigtown, BG9 7HJ
VAT Registration No 119 0799 52

INVOICE NO 2017

Date: 18 May 20XX

Campbell Kitchens
47 Landsway Road
Stotton
ST4 9TX

	£
Supplying goods for re-sale	2,146.80
VAT @ 20%	429.36
Total for payment	2,576.16
Terms: 30 days	

Purchase credit note

Vanstone plc
404 Larchway Estate, Brigtown, BG9 7HJ
VAT Registration No 119 0799 52

CREDIT NOTE NO 426

Linked to INVOICE NO 417

Date: 20 May 20XX

Campbell Kitchens
47 Landsway Road
Stotton
ST4 9TX

	£
Return of goods supplied for re-sale	612.75
VAT @ 20%	122.55
Total for payment	735.30
Terms: 30 days	

Task 6a

Refer to the following cash sales listing and enter these into the accounting software.

Date	Payment method	Details	Amount
5 May 20XX	Cheque	A Davis – kitchen equipment	£375 including VAT
12 May 20XXX	Cash	P Kowalksi – kitchen furniture	£120 including VAT
17 May 20XX	Cash	M Ahmed - kitchen equipment	£74 including VAT
24 May 20XX	Cheque	JL Green – kitchen equipment	£474 including VAT

Task 6b

Refer to the following email from Kitty Campbell and enter this transaction into the accounting software.

Email

From: Kitty Campbell
To: Accounting Technician
Date: 10 May 20XX
Subject: Premises insurance

Hello

I have today paid our annual premises insurance of £819.40 by business debit card.

Please record this transaction. VAT is not applicable.

Thanks,
Kitty

Task 7

Refer to the following BACS remittance advice notes received from customers and enter these transactions into the accounting software, ensuring you allocate all amounts as stated on each remittance advice note.

SCL Interiors
BACS Remittance Advice

To: Campbell Kitchens   15 May 20XX

An amount of £1,906.50 has been paid directly into your bank account in payment of the balance outstanding at 1 May.

Fry and Partners
BACS Remittance Advice

To: Campbell Kitchens   25 May 20XX

An amount of £1,097.44 has been paid directly into your bank account in payment of the balance outstanding at 1 May and including credit note 61.

Task 8

Refer to the following summary of cheque payments made to suppliers. Enter these transactions into the accounting software, ensuring you allocate (where applicable) all amounts shown in the details column.

Cheques paid listing

Date 20XX	Cheque number	Supplier	£	Details
12 May	006723	Vanstone plc	1,200.00	Payment on account
24 May	006724	Hart Ltd	1,012.75	Payment of opening balance
31 May	006725	Jackson Builders	456.35	Payment of opening balance

Task 9

Refer to the following standing order schedule and:

(a) set up a recurring entry for rent standing order schedule below.

(b) save a screen shot of the screen, setting up the recurring entry prior to processing. You will be provided with required evidence number for this in Task 13.

(c) process the first payment.

Standing order schedule

Details	Amount	Frequency of payment	Total no. of payments	Payment start date 20XX	Payment finish date 20XX
Rent – VAT N/A	£750	One payment every 2 months	3	2 May	2 September

Task 10

(a) Refer to the following petty cash vouchers and enter these into the accounting software.

Petty Cash Reimbursement	
PCR No 29	
Date: 1 May 20XX Cash from the bank account to restore the petty cash account to £150.00.	£81.76

(b) Refer to the following petty cash vouchers and enter these transactions into the computer.

Petty Cash Voucher	
Date 7 May 20XX PC212	**No**
Printer paper – including VAT Receipt attached	£ 45.60

Petty Cash Voucher	
Date 18 May 20XX PC213	**No**
Rail fare VAT not applicable Receipt attached	£ 37.90

Task 11

Refer to the following journal entries and enter them into the accounting software.

JOURNAL ENTRIES – 24 May 20XX	£	£
Premises insurance	10.00	
Bank		10.00
Being an error in the amount shown on Kitty Campbell's email of 10 May for premises insurance		

JOURNAL ENTRIES – 24 May 20XX	£	£
Drawings	600.00	
Bank		600.00
Being cash withdrawn from the bank by Kitty Campbell for personal use		

Task 12

Refer to the following bank statement. Using the accounting software and the transactions you have already posted:

(a) Enter any additional items on the bank statement that have yet to be recorded, into the accounting software (ignore VAT on any of these transactions).

(b) Reconcile the bank statement. If the bank statement does not reconcile, check your work and make the necessary corrections.

(c) Save a screenshot of the bank reconciliation screen. You will be provided with the required evidence number for this in Task 13.

Rowley Bank plc
505 High Street
Stotton
ST1 9VG

Campbell Kitchens
47 Landsway Road
Stotton
ST4 9TX

Account number 62082176

31 May 20XX

STATEMENT OF ACCOUNT

Date 20XX	Details	Paid out £	Paid in £	Balance £
01 May	Opening balance			4,916.26C
01 May	Cash	81.76		4,834.50C
02 May	James Holdings Ltd – Rent	750.00		4,084.50C
05 May	Counter credit		375.00	4,459.50C
10 May	FH Insurance plc	829.40		3,630.10C
12 May	Cheque 006723	1,200.00		2,430.10C
12 May	Counter credit		120.00	2,550.10C
15 May	BACS – SCL Interiors		1,906.50	4,456.60C
17 May	Counter credit		74.00	4,530.60C
24 May	Cash withdrawn	600.00		3,930.60C
25 May	BACS – Fry and Partners		1,097.44	5,028.04C
28 May	Bank interest received		24.20	5,052.24C
30 May	Counter credit		474.00	5,526.24C
29 May	Bank charges	15.00		5,511.24C
	D = Debit C = Credit			

Task 13

Documentation of evidence

You are now required to generate the following documents to demonstrate your competence:

Document and reports	Save/upload as:
A document showing all customer invoices during May 20XX	File name = Evidence 1a – Name – AAT Number
A document showing the balance owed by each customer as at 31 May 20XX	File name = Evidence 1b – Name – AAT Number
The following information must be evidenced within these documents: • Customer name • Account code • Payment terms	Depending on your software you may need to save one or more documents.
A document showing all supplier invoices during May 20XX	File name = Evidence 2a – Name – AAT Number
A document showing the balance owed to each supplier as at 31 May 20XX	File name = Evidence 2b – Name – AAT Number
The following information must be evidenced within these documents: • Supplier name • Account code • Payment terms	Depending on your software you may need to save one or more documents.
Audit trail, showing full details of all transactions, including details of receipts/payments allocated to items in customer/supplier accounts and details in the bank account that have been reconciled .	File name = Evidence 3 – Name – AAT Number
Trial Balance as at 31 May 20XX	File name = Evidence 4 – Name – AAT Number

Document and reports	Save/upload as:
A screenshot of the recurring entry screen including all relevant input details.	File name = Evidence 5 – Name – AAT Number
A screenshot of the bank reconciliation screen showing the reconciled items.	File name = Evidence 6 – Name – AAT Number

BPP PRACTICE ASSESSMENT 2
Using Accounting Software

ANSWERS

Using Accounting Software
BPP practice assessment 2

Some answers are given below, although these are not exhaustive. The answers provided are indicative of relevant content within the audit trail, the exact format of which will differ according to the computerised accounting package used.

Task	Transaction type	Account(s)	Date 20XX	Net Amount £	VAT £	Allocated against receipt/ payment ✓	Reconciled with bank statement ✓
1	Customer O/bal	FRA001	01 May	2,017.60			
	Customer O/bal	FRY002	01 May	1,597.60		✓	
	Customer O/bal	SCL001	01 May	1,906.50		✓	
2	Supplier O/bal	HAR001	01 May	1,012.75		✓	
	Supplier O/bal	JAC001	01 May	456.35			
	Supplier O/bal	VAN001	01 May	2,097.40			
3	Debit	Motor vehicles	01 May	20,067.10			
	Debit	Bank current account	01 May	4,916.26			✓
	Debit	Petty cash	01 May	68.24			
	Credit	VAT on sales	01 May	1,497.68			
	Debit	VAT on purchases	01 May	909.23			
	Credit	Capital	01 May	26,416.85			
	Debit	Drawings	01 May	350.00			
	Credit	Sales – kitchen furniture	01 May	456.20			
	Credit	Sales – kitchen equipment	01 May	119.30			
	Debit	Goods for re-sale	01 May	224.00			
	Debit	Sales ledger control*	01 May	5,521.70			
	Credit	Purchases ledger control*	01 May	3,566.50			
		*If appropriate					

Task	Transaction type	Account(s)		Date 20XX	Net Amount £	VAT £	Allocated against receipt/ payment ✓	Reconciled with bank statement ✓
4	Sales inv	FRY002	Sales – Kitchen furniture	07 May	1,676.40	335.28		
	Sales inv	FRA001	Sales – Kitchen equip	21 May	710.20	142.04		
	Sales inv	SCL001	Sales – Kitchen furniture	23 May	1,249.17	249.83		
	Sales inv	FRY002	Sales – Kitchen furniture	27 May	446.17	89.23		
	Sales CN	FRY002	Sales – Kitchen furniture	14 May	416.80	83.36	✓	
5	Purchases inv	JAC001	Repairs	12 May	909.25	181.85		
	Purchases inv	VAN001	Goods	18 May	2,146.80	429.36		
	Purchases CN	VAN001	Goods	20 May	612.75	122.55		
6a	Bank receipt (Other receipt in Sage One)	Bank	Sales – Kitchen equip	5 May	312.50	62.50		✓
	Bank/Other receipt	Bank	Sales – Kitchen furniture	12 May	100.00	20.00		✓
	Bank/Other receipt	Bank	Sales – Kitchen equip	17 May	61.67	12.33		✓
	Bank/Other receipt	Bank	Sales – Kitchen equip	24 May	395.00	79.00		✓
6b	Bank payment	Bank	Premises insurance	10 May	819.40			✓
7	Customer receipt	SCL001	Bank	15 May	1906.50			✓
	Customer receipt	FRY002	Bank	25 May	1097.44			✓
8	Supplier payment on a/c	VAN001	Bank	12 May	1,200.00			✓
	Supplier payment	HAR001	Bank	24 May	1,012.75			
	Supplier payment	JAC001	Bank	27 May	456.35			
9	Bank payment	Bank	Rent – SO/DD	02 May	750.00			✓

Task	Transaction type	Account(s)		Date 20XX	Net Amount £	VAT £	Allocated against receipt/ payment ✓	Reconciled with bank statement ✓
10	Dr	Petty cash		01 May	81.76			
	Cr	Bank		01 May	81.76			✓
	Cash payment	Petty cash	Stationery	07 May	38.00	7.60		
	Cash payment	Petty cash	Travel	18 May	37.90			
11	Journal debit	Insurance		24 May	10.00			
	Journal credit	Bank		24 May	10.00			✓
	Journal debit	Drawings		24 May	600.00			
	Journal credit	Bank		24 May	600.00			✓
12	Bank/Other receipt	Bank	Bank interest received	28 May	24.20			✓
	Bank/Other payment	Bank	Bank charges	28 May	15.00			✓

Additional guidance for individual tasks

If you struggled with the assessment, we suggest you read the guidance below and attempt the assessment again. Note that when we refer to 'Sage' in this section, this covers both Sage 50 and Sage One, unless otherwise stated.

Task 1 (guidance)

All customers listed should be set up. Be careful to set them up as customers rather than suppliers. Enter the dates and opening balances carefully, as you will lose marks for inaccuracies. In Sage, when you enter the opening balances for customers, this creates a **debit to the sales ledger account** and a **credit to a suspense account**. When you enter either a debit or credit in each of Tasks 1 to 3 using the opening balance options within Sage, the opposite side of the entry will be posted to a suspense account. However, as the debits and credits you are given in the assessment are equal, the debits and credits to the suspense account will cancel each other off to a nil value, **if you have entered all opening balances correctly.** If you are left with a suspense account balance, then you will have made a mistake while entering the balances.

Note that if you are using Sage One, you need to enter the opening balance date as **30 April 20XX** as the program requires it to be one day before the accounts start date. Other programs, including Sage 50, may allow you to enter the opening balance date as 1 May 20XX.

••

BPP
LEARNING MEDIA

Task 2 (guidance)

It is important that you set up all **suppliers** listed and that you set them up as suppliers, rather than customers. Enter the dates and opening balances carefully and check that all of your entries match the information you have been given.

Note that if you are using Sage One, you need to enter the opening balance date as **30 April 20XX,** as the program requires it to be one day before the accounts start date. Other programs, including Sage 50, may allow you to enter the opening balance date as 1 May 20XX.

Task 3 (guidance)

Most of these accounts will already be on Sage, so you just need to enter the opening balances for these. However, for some accounts, you will need to either create new accounts or amend the names of existing accounts.

Be careful when entering the balances and selecting the appropriate nominal accounts to make entries to.

When you have finished entering the data, check you have not missed any accounts by previewing a trial balance. Remember – if you have a balance on the suspense account, then you have entered something incorrectly.

Note that if you are using Sage One, you need to enter the opening balance date as **30 April 20XX** as the program requires it to be one day before the accounts start date. Other programs, including Sage 50, may allow you to enter the opening balance date as 1 May 20XX.

Task 4 (guidance)

Both invoices and the credit note in the listings need to be entered carefully, ensuring you don't enter the credit note as an invoice, as you will be in the habit of posting invoices by the time you get to it. It is very important to select the correct nominal account if you want to score well in this task. Always check you have entered **all** of the transactions.

Task 5 (guidance)

When posting purchase invoices/credit notes, make sure you select the right supplier and an appropriate nominal account. Make sure you have accounted for the VAT properly too. Always check you have entered **all** of the transactions.

Task 6a and 6b (guidance)

This task requires you to process payments and receipts that are not related to credit transactions with customers or suppliers. You should use the Other Payment/Other Receipt function in Sage One or the Bank Payment/Bank Receipt function in Sage 50.

Ensure you use the right way of accounting for VAT for cash sales. You are only given the gross amount. Therefore, in Sage One, you should enter the gross amount, and the program will automatically calculate and post the VAT. In Sage 50, although it may seem odd, firstly enter the gross amount in the Net field. Then press F9 and the program will automatically calculate the net amount.

As always, the choice of nominal account is important. Be careful not to omit any payments or receipts.

Tasks 7 and 8 (guidance)

When entering supplier payments or customer receipts using Sage, you should use the **Supplier Payment** or **Customer Receipt** functions (not the Bank Payment or Bank Receipt functions (Other Payment/Other Receipt functions in Sage One) as demonstrated earlier in this Text. You should find this makes it easy to allocate the payment/receipt to the correct supplier/ customer account. Don't miss out any transactions.

Task 9 (guidance)

Recurring payments are a bit tricky in Sage 50 – when you first enter the details, they do not impact on the nominal ledger. When you go back into Recurring items in Sage 50 to process the payment, remember **you only need to process the first payment.**

For Sage One however, the process is a bit different. You create and post the first payment using the **Other Payment** function. You then go back into the payment to set up the recurrence.

Details on how to do this were covered in Chapter 2/Chapter 4 of this Text.

Note that you are required to take a screen print in this task and you can do this by pressing **Print Screen** or **PrtScn (or PrtSc).**

In Sage One, take a screenshot of both the 'Other Payment' screen with the details of the first payment, and the 'Make Recurring' screen with details of the recurrence.

In Sage 50 take a screenshot of the Add/Edit recurring entry screen with details of the first payment and recurrence.

Task 10 (guidance)

You must remember to change the nominal code in Sage 50 to the Petty Cash (called 'Cash' in Sage One) nominal code when entering the payments in this task.

You can use the **Bank Transfer** button in Sage for the payment from the Bank current account to the Petty cash account.

Task 11 (guidance)

Enter journals carefully to ensure you debit and credit the correct accounts. Don't get the debits and credits mixed up.

Task 12 (guidance)

Having entered the bank charges and bank interest received, you should reconcile the bank using the method covered in Chapter 2/Chapter 4.

In the answer provided, you can see which items you should have reconciled as they appear in the 'Matched transactions' section in the bottom half of the bank reconciliation screen in Sage 50. In Sage One, the reconciled items have a tick in 'Reconciled' column in the bank reconciliation screen.

Take a screenshot of the bank reconciliation screen just before you save the reconciliation (ie, before you click on Save button in Sage One, or the 'Reconcile' button in Sage 50).

Task 13 (guidance)

This task tests your ability to generate the reports specified. You will get the marks available for this particular task by **generating the correct report**. You will receive these marks even if some of the transactions within the report are incorrect because you entered them incorrectly in earlier tasks.

There is a comprehensive section on generating reports in Chapter 2/Chapter 4 of this Text. You should look back at this if you were unable to generate and save as PDF files, any reports. **Make sure you check that you have saved all the reports**.

Specific guidance for each document/report is given below in **bold**.

Document and reports	Save / upload as:
Ensure you specify the correct date/date range for all reports:	**For the purpose of this practice assessment, save the documents to your desktop on your computer. In a real assessment you would also be required to upload these documents, but ignore the step of uploading for this practice assessment.**
A document showing all customer invoices during May 20XX	
Run the 'Day Books: Customer Invoices (Detailed)' report in Sage 50.	File name = Evidence 1a – Name – AAT Number
In Sage One, run the Sales Day Book report.	
A document showing the balance owed by each customer as at 31 May 20XX	
Run the 'Aged Debtors Analysis – Detailed' report in Sage 50, or the 'Aged Debtors' report in Sage One and click the 'Detailed' button.	File name = Evidence 1b – Name – AAT Number
The following information must be evidenced within these documents:	Depending on your software you may need to save one or more documents.
• Customer name • Account code • Payment terms	**Name these in the same way as above, continuing the sequence, eg, Evidence 1c...**
You need a separate document for payment terms – a screenshot of the Customer Record screen for each customer in Sage One. For Sage 50, you need the Credit Control screen within each Customer Record.	

Document and reports	Save / upload as:
A document showing all supplier invoices during May 20XX **Run the 'Day Books: Supplier Invoices (Detailed)' report in Sage 50.** **In Sage One, run the 'Purchases Day Book' report.**	File name = **Evidence 2a – Name – AAT Number**
A document showing the balance owed to each supplier as at 31 May 20XX **Run the 'Aged Creditors Analysis – Detailed' report in Sage 50, or the 'Aged Creditors' report in Sage One and click the 'Detailed' button.** *The following information must be evidenced within these documents:* • Supplier name • Account code • Payment terms **You need a separate document for payment terms – a screenshot of the Supplier Record screen for each supplier in Sage One. For Sage 50, you need the Credit Control screen within each Supplier Record**	File name = **Evidence 2b – Name – AAT Number** Depending on your software you may need to save one or more documents.
Audit trail, showing full details of all transactions, including details of receipts/payments allocated to items in customer/supplier accounts and details in the bank account that have been reconciled **Run the 'Audit Trail – Detailed' report.** **To show bank reconciled items:**	File name = **Evidence 3 – Name – AAT Number**

Document and reports	Save / upload as:
Sage 50 - reconciled items have an 'R' in the 'B' column of the report. *Sage One - ensure the report is configured to include 'Bank Reconciled' column. Reconciled items have a tick in this column.* **To show receipts/payments allocated to items in customer/supplier accounts:** *Sage 50 - the report indicates the invoices that receipts/payments are allocated to, eg, '24.42 to PI 4' shows that a payment of 24.42 is allocated to purchase invoice no. 4.* *Sage One - use the Customer/Supplier Activity reports generated in 1a and 2a above. Allocated items are identified by having 0.00 in the 'Outstanding' column)*	
Trial Balance as at 31 May 20XX **Run the 'Trial balance' report**	File name = **Evidence 4 – Name – AAT Number**
A screenshot of the recurring entry screen including all relevant input details. **From Task 9b** **In Sage One, take a screenshot of both the 'Other Payment' screen with the details of the first payment, and the 'Create Recurring Payment' screen with details of the recurrence.** **In Sage 50 take a screenshot of the Add/Edit recurring entry screen with details of the first payment and recurrence.**	File name = **Evidence 5 – Name – AAT Number**

Document and reports	Save / upload as:
A screenshot of the bank reconciliation screen showing the reconciled items . **From Task 12b** **Take a screenshot of the bank reconciliation screen just before you save the reconciliation (ie, before you click on Save button in Sage One and Reconcile button in Sage 50)**	File name = **Evidence 6 – Name – AAT Number**

Index

P

Payments, 50, 51, 59, 138, 139, 147
PDF, 4, 94
Petty cash, 64, 154
Print screen, 5, 94
Program date, 35, 46, 134
Purchase invoices, 36, 121
Purchases and Purchases Returns Day Books, 77

R

Receipts, 50, 51, 57, 58, 70, 138, 147
Recurring payments, 61, 151
Reports, 72, 77, 80, 159
Restore files, 10

S

Sales and Sales Returns Day Books, 77
Sales invoices, 41, 42, 127

Screenshots, 5, 94
Standing orders, 61, 151
Statements, 75, 164
Supplier, 25, 88, 111, 175
Supplier account, 26, 112
Supplier codes, 25, 111
Supplier invoices, 36, 121
Supplier payments, 51, 139
Supplier record, 88, 175
Supplier report, 74, 175

T

Tax codes, 20, 21, 46, 108, 110
Trade creditors ledger, 25, 88, 122, 175
Trade debtors ledger, 88, 111, 123, 175
Trial balance, 78, 81, 170

V

VAT, 14, 20, 21, 46, 108, 110, 134

REVIEW FORM

How have you used this Combined Text and Question Bank?
(Tick one box only)

☐ Home study

☐ On a course_____

☐ Other _____

Why did you decide to purchase this Combined Text and Question Bank?
(Tick one box only)

☐ Have used BPP Texts in the past

☐ Recommendation by friend/colleague

☐ Recommendation by a college lecturer

☐ Saw advertising

☐ Other _____

During the past six months do you recall seeing/receiving either of the following?
(Tick as many boxes as are relevant)

☐ Our advertisement in Accounting Technician

☐ Our Publishing Catalogue

Which (if any) aspects of our advertising do you think are useful?
(Tick as many boxes as are relevant)

☐ Prices and publication dates of new editions

☐ Information on Text content

☐ Details of our free online offering

☐ None of the above

Your ratings, comments and suggestions would be appreciated on the following areas of this Combined Text and Question Bank.

	Very useful	Useful	Not useful
Introductory section	☐	☐	☐
Quality of explanations	☐	☐	☐
Chapter tasks	☐	☐	☐
Assessments	☐	☐	☐
Test your learning	☐	☐	☐
Index	☐	☐	☐

	Excellent	Good	Adequate	Poor
Overall opinion of this publication	☐	☐	☐	☐

Do you intend to continue using BPP products? ☐ Yes ☐ No

Please note any further comments and suggestions/errors on the reverse of this page.

The BPP author of this edition can be emailed at: learningmedia@bpp.com

REVIEW FORM (continued)

TELL US WHAT YOU THINK

Please note any further comments and suggestions/errors below